People of the Lane

Dedicated to the People of the Lane
Past, Present and Future

© Dr. Kay Flavell 2021
Published by New Pacific Studio
Book design by Design Site, Berkeley
Printed by Biddles, King's Lynn, Norfolk PE32 1 SF http://www.biddles.co.uk
Front cover: 'Lark Lane at 6am,' 2019, courtesy of Caroline Oates
Back cover: 'Sefton Park after rain,' 2019. KF

New Pacific Studio Vallejo
321 Nevada St.
Vallejo CA 94590
USA
www.newpacificstudio.org

978-0-578-70934-5

All rights reserved. No part of this publication may be reproduced, stored in a retrieval system, or transmitted in any form or by any means, electronic, mechanical, photocopying, recording or otherwise, without prior permission from the publisher.

People of the Lane

Living in and around
Lark Lane, 1880-2020

Kay Flavell

with photographs by
Tom Wood

Previous page: Aerial view of Lark Lane and Sefton Park showing downtown Liverpool and the River Mersey. The Lane starts to the left of the tennis courts in centre right. *Above:* Sefton Park Lake at 6am.
Following page: Aerial photo of Lark Lane.

Contents

Foreword by Bryan Biggs .... *x*
Preface .... *xii*

I   A Brief History of the Lane, 1880-1980 1

II   People of the Lane: Interviews, 1980-81 25
        - Mrs. Margaret McLean 'It's such a long story' 25
        - Working on the Lane 33
        - Six Older Residents 116
        - Growing up in the Big Houses 125
        - Institutions 151

III   Growing up around the Lane, 1940-1980 169
        - Stories from Ten Streets 172

IV   Global Village: The Lane Today, 2020 241
        - During the Pandemic 243

V   Postscript: Reimagining Liverpool 259

Subscribers to Lark Lane Telephone Exchange, 1899 265
List of interviewees and online contributors 271
Illustration Credits 276
Bibliography 278
About the Photographer 283
About the Author 285
About the Designer 287
Acknowledgements 288
Map 289

Foreword

Lark Lane, as one of the people interviewed in this book suggests, epitomises Liverpool. When Kay Flavell conducted her study four decades ago, this unassuming street, located between tranquil Sefton Park and Aigburth Road's busy dual carriageway, reflected something of the declining fortunes the port was then experiencing. The mercantile and shipping wealth once associated with the big houses in the surrounding leafy streets had long gone. The faded grandeur of the neighbourhood could not disguise the acute economic and social impact being felt across Merseyside as it bore the brunt of neoliberal government policies and the legacies of Britain's post-industrialisation. Yet many of the old independent shops and businesses on the Lane remained, while new blood and entrepreneurialism were re-energising an already existing and deeply-held sense of community. In the words of another interviewee, Lark Lane then, as now, can feel 'more like a country village than a town street'.

The new wine bar and restaurants, antique and book shops, and the transient young population occupying bed-sits in those grand merchants' houses, had brought new life to the Lane, despite concerns over 'too many trendies'. By the early 1980s it was vibrant during both night and day, a social and creative hub that sat comfortably alongside its function as a shopping street. While the popular media image of Liverpool at this time is one of irreversible decline and municipal catastrophe, it was a period that also witnessed a cultural flowering, especially in music. Many post-punk, psychedelically-inclined Liverpool bands enjoyed cult success through performing in 'Larks in the Park,' one of whose co-founders was a Lark Lane resident interviewed here.

Kay has managed to capture life on the Lane through a wonderful collection of personal stories of lives and livelihoods, memories and aspirations. Included are stories from shopkeepers, restaurateurs, pub landlords, hairdressers, an antique dealer, bookseller, acupuncturist, upholsterer, chemist, garage-owner, butcher, builder, vicar and shoe-repairer, alongside residents of the neighbourhood for whom Lark Lane provides their daily focus. From this oral history snapshot we glimpse changing social attitudes and values, providing a microcosm of Liverpool's, and also of Britain's, shifting social fabric. There are intergenerational perspectives too, encompassing memories of turn-of-the-century semi-rural suburbia, an era of dairies and cattle, servants and chauffeurs, trams and a telephone exchange, right through to Liverpool's first suburban French restaurant and wine bar, the arrival of a democratic café society and community organisation.

All of Kay's interviewees express a fondness for the Lane. Some had enjoyed life-long careers or built successful businesses there, others had just arrived with high hopes, others still had survived war or economic hardship. There are reflections on the disappearance of an old world of deference, the slow erosion of stratified class. Some of the stories told by those who rarely left the area are remarkable in what they reveal from day-to-day experiences, while others recall foreign adventure or talk of the possibilities for a new spiritual age. The life of the Lane is construed as one of stability and transience, its stories both fixed and fluid.

I had the good fortune to live on the Lane myself for a brief time, residing in a flat at the corner of Hadassah Grove. I frequented Keith's wine bar and the record fairs held at the Old Police Station. I can put a face to several of the voices in this book, people I have known, including one who has passed away.

Recently, not for old time's sake but as relief from the restrictions of Coronavirus lockdown, I have been visiting Lark Lane at least once a week on circular evening walks that take me to the river and back. The Lane is now deserted, closed for business except for a couple of restaurants doing take-aways. But in the eerie silence and absence of people, traffic and aromas from the many eating places that have sprung up in recent years, the lives of the people whose words are recorded here, along with Tom Wood's vivid photographs, remind me of the richness of the life that will return.

Bryan Biggs, Director of Cultural Legacies, Bluecoat. June 12, 2020

Preface

People of the Lane is a mosaic of voices and faces, recording moments in the life stories of more than eighty contributors. Its aim is to honour the strength, resilience and sense of humour displayed in the drama of everyday life by members of this Liverpool community. I had the good fortune to live for a year beside the Lane, and that experience turned me into a lifelong story collector. Thank you, my friends!

The main section of interviews was recorded on tapes in 1980-81 and transcribed between then and 1983. Tom Wood's wonderful photographs were also made in those years. The earliest memories of several older residents date back to the 1880s, when Sefton Park and the shops along the Lane were just becoming established. Some stories record growing up in the big houses, others in the terraced houses. They all shared the Park and the Lane. After a short history of the Lane in Part 1, we start listening to voices with the story of Aunt Maggie (Mrs. Margaret McLean), aged 93, in Part II.

The third section of the book dates from 2019-2020, when work on the book resumed after a 40-year hiatus. Via a Facebook page, 'People from around Lark Lane,' set up by Lark Laner Dave Turton, current and former residents were invited to contribute memories of growing up around the Lane between 1940-1980.

The final section on the Lane in 2020 brings us forward to the present, and shows the interwoven lives of people on the Lane and in many other countries. We face the fears and tragedies of the COVID-19 pandemic no matter where we live in our global village. And we live in hope.

KF, New Pacific Studio. April 17, 2020

Overleaf: Lark Lane in the 1940s.

Liver bird crest on the Old Police Station, Lark Lane.

I | A BRIEF HISTORY OF THE LANE, 1880-1980

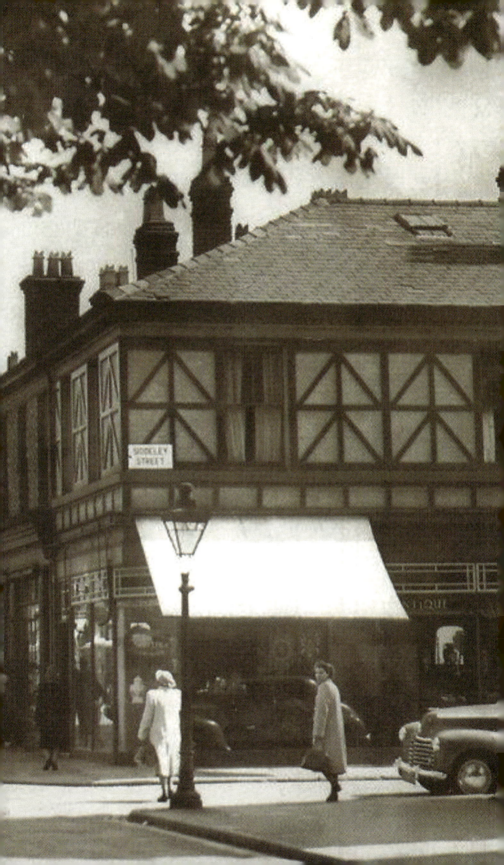

I   A BRIEF HISTORY OF THE LANE

Introduction (1983)

People of the Lane highlights moments in the growth and decline of the old community of Lark Lane, and shows how a new community has established itself in the shops and houses of the older urban village. It is based upon a series of taped interviews carried out in 1980-81, before the riots of the summer of 1981 in nearby Toxteth briefly focused national attention upon the severe problems of Liverpool's inner-city areas. Lark Lane has its share of these problems, but it also has a strong sense of community and a faith in the gradual processes of urban renewal.

Lark Lane now has a reputation as one of the liveliest areas of Liverpool. This is especially true on Sundays, when the wine bars and pubs, antique shops and bookshop all do a good trade with people who come to walk in Sefton Park, or just to browse on the Lane itself. The antique fairs and regular craft fairs held in the Old Police Station, which now houses the Lark Lane and St. Michael's Community Association, constantly bring in new faces.

This area on the edge of the inner city cherishes its blend of old and new and creates a strong sense of belonging, not just in those born in the area, but also in relative newcomers. The narrow pavements and the smallness of the shops encourage personal contact, and shopping here still involves patience and a love of the art of conversation.

At the same time, it is also an area of severe urban decay where large brick Victorian villas, subdivided into a dozen or more bed-sitters, are gradually left to rot, their plumbing and roofs untended and their front gardens littered with overflowing dustbins, abandoned cars or trees grown too big for their site. This is part of the physical heritage of the past, whose housing patterns cannot be easily or cheaply adapted to modern needs. On the positive side, housing associations and conservation societies have brought new hope to the area, and community associations have proved tenacious in fighting off attempts by city planners to go ahead with demolition against the wishes of the local inhabitants.

My primary concern is with Lark Lane as a shopping street and its everyday routines. So I start with the shopkeepers themselves, asking how long they have been part of the Lane. How do they view, as well as contribute to, its changing character? Next come the voices of residents spanning the decades from 1880 on.

To some extent, changes on the Lane mirror broader changes in class relations during this period. The Victorian Lane reflected the master and servant relationships of the rest of society. The 'high class' shops of the area received that name because they were providing for the needs of a middle class and upper middle class living in the surrounding big houses. Today, these distinctions have been eroded, a change that is welcomed by some and regretted by others, according to their social and political convictions. I record their different viewpoints. At the same time, I share the view of many members of the new community that the unusually good social mix of the area is a source of its vitality and will ensure its survival.

The Growth of the Lane, 1880-1914

Up to the middle of the nineteenth century Lark Lane was just a narrow lane in the green countryside lying beyond the Dingle, running at a right angle to Park Lane, later to be renamed Aigburth Road, which was the main thoroughfare out to Aigburth. Aigburth itself, originally Ackeberth, the place of many oaks, apparently derived its name from a druidical sacred grove. This area also fell within the limits of Toxteth Park, the ancient hunting park of King John. There were two lodges within its boundaries, the upper lodge giving its name to Lodge Lane, and the lower lodge in Otterspool. Lark Lane seems to go back to around 1800, and the earliest settlement off it was in Hadassah Grove, which was settled in the first half of the century and remained a private road, sealed off from the Lane by gates which were locked regularly in the morning and evening.

To the left of Lark Lane lay the Parkfield estate owned by Robert Gladstone and later by Charles Tayleur, who in 1858 had Parkfield Road cut through his land. The enormous commercial expansion of Liverpool created a demand for good middle-class housing with larger gardens than the older handsome terraces around Falkner Square could provide, and new villas began to be built along Ullet Road and Parkfield Road.

In 1847 Birkenhead Park, designed by Joseph Paxton and his team, opened on the other side of the Mersey, in the small town of Birkenhead. This new public park of 226 acres quickly won local and international acclaim for its garden design, ceremonial gates and buildings. In 1850 it was visited and greatly admired by Frederick Law Olmsted, future designer of Central Park in New York. Local and international interest in designing central city parks to promote the health and leisure needs of rapidly expanding urban populations of all classes no doubt spurred Liverpool Corporation to pursue similar city improvements. A primary role was played by the visionary young merchant Charles Pierre Melly (1829-1888), who was elected a city councillor in 1866. Charles had a cosmopolitan education and was familiar with Geneva, birthplace of his father André Melly. Charles married his Swiss cousin Louise in Geneva in 1854, just at the time when the famous English Garden was being developed there.

Charles Melly came up with the original vision of Sefton Park and chaired the parks and gardens committee during the years the park was being formed. 235 acres lying outside the city boundaries was purchased from the Earl of Sefton, with the plan of developing the area as the site of a large metropolitan park. It would be ringed by large leasehold mansions, which would appeal to the merchants and professional classes of the growing city. An international competition was held, won by a partnership between Liverpool architect Lewis Hornblower and the head gardener of the parks of Paris, Edouard André. Charles Melly commissioned grottoes and acted as host for the French gardening team.

Lithograph celebrating the 1872 opening of Sefton Park.

Sefton Park was opened by the young Prince Arthur in May 1872. Over the next thirty years, the fashionable middle classes relocated from cramped older houses in the inner city to larger houses and gardens built around Aigburth Drive and in the streets to the left and right of Lark Lane. On the other side of the park in the Mossley Hill area were the mansions of the Holt, Melly and Rathbone families.

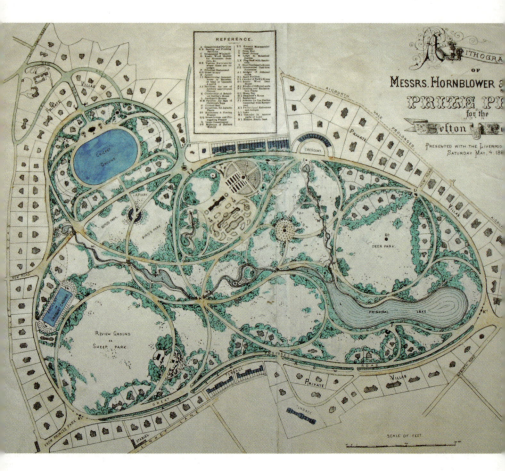

Sefton Park Hornblower plan.

The Lane itself developed from the late 1860s onwards as the natural heart of this new district. By around 1900, it offered a range of what were considered 'high-class shops', along with a post office and sorting office, a fire station, a police station, and a free public lending library. In 1895 the whole area was brought within the city boundaries.

It was a mixed community, with members of the middle classes and the working classes living in close proximity. In the 1880s investors built two-up, two-down brick terraced houses with outhouses to the right of the Lane in Hesketh Street, Bickerton Street, Lucerne Street and Siddeley Street. These provided rental accommodation for small tradesmen and for others who earned their living by doing domestic work, chimney-sweeping, gardening and working as casual labourers in 'the big houses,' as they are still called. Most working-class children spent their school years from the ages five to fourteen at the Board school of St. Michael's, which opened on the far side of Aigburth Road in 1890. After leaving school, they began to work locally, either in trade apprenticeships or in private service. Some went to sea or worked on the docks, but this was never the main source of employment in the area.

During the period from 1880 until the outbreak of the First World War, Liverpool felt confident of its future. In the *Liberal Review* for 1878, published weekly at the cost of one penny, a writer contrasted the expanded *Gore's Directory* of 1878 with the 1766 volume, and commented hopefully 'There is no reason to doubt that Liverpool will increase in population and importance in the future in something like the same ratio as it has done in the past.'

Then as now, living conditions were vastly better for the middle classes than for most working-class families. Public criticisms of the city for its neglect of the poorer sections of the community were usually countered either by pointing to the city's record for promoting charities, or by implying that the 'suffering and misery' associated with poverty were caused not by starvation wages, but were a result of 'vice'. In other words, instead of discussing the economic situation of large segments of the working classes dependent upon casual labour and the gap between their earnings and their basic needs, poor families were frequently blamed for their poverty and criminalised. Members of the middle class, by contrast, were praised for seeking to 'reclaim the vicious':

> Liverpool, in common with all crowded centers of population, has plenty of vice, suffering and misery in its midst, but it also has noble agencies for reclaiming the vicious, remedying the suffering, and ameliorating the misery. *(The Liberal Review, 1878, p. 10)*

Merchants' wives and unmarried daughters were expected to devote their leisure to charitable causes. Their husbands made the money and paid low wages, while their wives redistributed some of the surplus in the form of charity. A late nineteenth century social register, B. Guinness Orchard's *Liverpool's Legion of Honour* (1893), gives long biographies of the men, but grants only a single line to their wives, listing the various charities they supported.

Within the Lark Lane area, public education was conducted mainly by two institutions: the Board school, and the churches with their accompanying Sunday schools. For a while, Christ Church also ran a regular school at its red-brick Schools building opposite the Institute on the Lane. Mrs. Margaret McLean's older brothers went there, while she went to St. Michael-in-the-Hamlet. The Log Book of St. Michael's points to regular signs of friction between the headmaster and the rector of Christ Church.

Board schools were not normally attended by middle-class children. Ramsay Muir, the Liverpool historian who grew up in Birkenhead, comments 'Nobody who could afford any other kind of school sent their children to these places.' The better-off usually began with education at home conducted by a governess, or by attendance at one of the numerous dame's schools in the area, followed by the Liverpool College for boys or by the Liverpool High School, founded in 1880 and later renamed the Belvedere School, for girls.

Many boys tended to be sent away to public school; for girls, the pattern was to be sent away for a shorter term to be 'finished' at a boarding school. Elfreda Helen Cotton, née Moore, was born in Liverpool in 1892 and grew up in 1 Fulwood Park, just across Aigburth Road. Her education consisted of a governess, a year at a day school, three years at a boarding school in Suffolk, and six months at a finishing school in Paris. This pattern of going abroad was broken by the outbreak of the First World War and never resumed.

Church attendance absorbed a large part of Sunday. Mrs. Cotton would occasionally be taken by her mother Alice Rathbone, daughter of Philip H. Rathbone, to the Ancient Chapel of Toxteth at the bottom of Park Road. She found the services terribly long:

We used to go up in the gallery, where you would find yourself face to face with the minister, who was up on one of those three-tiered things. It was most alarming. I believe that when my mother went to the chapel as a child, she was allowed to take her own dolls' tea set with her, and was put in the bottom of one of the box pews. (Cotton, Recollections. Notes in PRO)

The large Church of England building of Christ Church, built in the decorated Gothic style, was opened in 1871 and soon boasted a regular congregation of around 800. The gentry used to attend the morning service, and the servants were expected to attend in the evening. The *Liverpool Review* for June 1886 gives this wry description of a Christ Church audience:

A typical specimen of a suburban church in which all the miserable sinners are fashionably dressed and sit in comfortably cushioned pews surrounded by all the luxuries that ecclesiastical art can furnish in the way of stained-glass windows and brass candelabra.

Another fashionable church built for the expanding population around the Park was the Presbyterian Sefton Park Church, founded in 1879.

It too held around 900 people, and was so popular that new members often had to wait for a year or more to obtain their own pew. Everyone paid pew rents. Dr. John Watson, famous for his Scottish novels written under the name of Ian Maclaren, was appointed minister there in 1880. He became so well known that tram conductors named the stop at Brompton Avenue 'Dr. John Watson's Church'. Services ran for two hours, with lengthy sermons, as Mr. Frank Camenisch notes below.

The congregation reflected the cosmopolitan nature of Liverpool's population: it included French, Germans, Swiss, Danes, Russians, Greeks, Austrians and Belgians. The Toxteth Congregationalist Church at the corner of Ullet Road opened in 1870, and the Roman Catholic Church of St. Charles Borromeo was established in 1900. It was supported by the international shipping de Larringa family and other families.

Who Lived around the Lane in the 1890s?

By the 1890s, most of the new building was completed. Mansions along the Drive and the big semi-detached houses to the left of the Lane were occupied by general merchants, cotton brokers, and shipping families, while terraced houses to the right of the Lane were home to a mixture of skilled and unskilled workmen and servants employed in the big houses. By 1900 a slow move away from Liverpool was already beginning — to the Wirral, or up the coast towards Southport. But a local man reported around 1900 that 'on the whole, the really old families cling to Aigburth and its neighbourhood'. A Fulwood Park address was 'suggestive of ultra-social importance', and Sefton Park could now claim 'some of the best-known families'.

Sefton Park entrance, c.1910.

Sefton Park model yacht race, 1896.

Aigburth Drive inhabitants included two members of a South American merchant family, G.W. Brocklehurst living at 'Olinda' and Henry B. Brocklehurst living in 'Sefton'. Other names include A. Ralli, J.H. Simpson of 'Annandale', general manager of the Bank of Liverpool, Thomas Chilton, chairman of the Phosphor Guano Company, the stockbroker Walter C. Clark of 'Orleans House', Mrs. Bowring in 'Terra Nova', and A.P. Fletcher, former chairman of the Runcorn Soap and Alkali Company. At No. 8 lived John Camenisch, a leading member of the Liverpool Cotton Exchange, which had been established in 1882. This house was later bequeathed to the University of Liverpool.

Families living in Livingston Drive around 1900 included F.C. Minoprio, a cotton merchant whose family moved from Frankfurt to

Liverpool, J.H. Clayton, another cotton broker, G.V. Morrell, who was in the provisions trade, and William Norman of 'The Lings', a general merchant. Alexandra Drive housed several members of the Dowdall family and other prominent figures were Louis Cohen, the general manager of Lewis's who lived at 'Ethelstone', Jose de Ybarrondo, James Calder, who was vice president of the Athenaeum Reading Room, and David Bingham, a corn merchant who was also a committee member of the popular Wellington Club. James Calder's wife Fanny Calder supported the Sandon Studio Society, which took up residence in the Bluecoat building in 1907, thus establishing the first arts centre in Liverpool and in the UK.

Most of the other roads housed a mixture of business and professional families. A cluster of street names – Waverley, Mannering, Marmion, and Ivanhoe – point to the popularity of Sir Walter Scott's novels at this time. Waverley Road was popular with university staff and at one time housed Oliver Lodge, Professor of Physics and famous for his work on extra-sensory perception, along with Henry S. Hele-Shaw, Professor of Engineering. Hargreaves Road had a typical mixture of occupations: the names here include William F. Gossage, a soap and soda maker whose brother Ernest lived in Marmion Road, John McGunn, a lecturer in philosophy, and Henry V. Weisse, headmaster of the Liverpool Institute, Mrs. Lloyd Rayner, who worked for the Ladies' Charity, John W. Wood, a maker of artificial limbs, and the Rev. John Burbridge, curate of St. Michael's. Oliver Elton, Professor of English, lived in Parkfield Road, along with Henry E. Rensburg, a stockbroker and keen amateur musician who moved to Liverpool from the Netherlands in 1863, and Vladimir Ouranofski, who held the splendid title of Imperial Vice Consul of Russia. He was later killed in his Rolls Royce.

One of the most colourful of the local residents was Miss Dora Yates, who devoted her life to the study and collection of gypsy lore. She came from an old, established, Liverpool Jewish family and was educated at Dr. T.W.M. Lund's private school in Croxteth Road. Her first interest in Romany culture was aroused by George Borrow's *The Bible in Spain*, which she was happily permitted to read on Sundays because her parents believed it was a devotional book.

Coach on the Lane outside the grocer Truesdale's, 1890s.

After taking a degree at the University of Liverpool, Dora taught for a while at the South Liverpool High School for girls in Alexandra Drive. She also worked in the university library, and helped to run the Gypsy Lore Society. After buying her own horse and caravan, under the name Rawnie Dorelia, Dora became a regular attender at the Nottingham Goose Fair and the Appleby Horse Fair. Material she collected was published in *A Book of Gypsy Folk Tales* (1948), and *My Gypsy Days* (1953). Her two sisters, Miss

Wilhelmina and Miss Katy Yates, ran a dame's school on the first floor above the stationers Sidley's, at the top of Lark Lane. This school later moved to Marmion Road, where it took the name of Camelot. Many of the older residents of the area began their schooldays there.

The Lane at Work, 1914-1939

This was the period during which most of the older inhabitants of the Lane were growing up. The social composition of the area did not change greatly during this period, although the gradual drift of the middle classes and very prosperous merchant families out of the inner city was already steadily increasing. Liverpool had already passed the peak of its prosperity and from 1918 was already on the decline. But the process was a gradual one, and there was still enough cheap domestic labour available to maintain the big houses. Those hardest hit by the depression years of the late '20s and '30s were the poorer off, especially men, who now found it much harder to gain casual employment on the docks or elsewhere.

Liverpool's Salthouse Dock in the era of sailing ships.

Working-class girls tended to leave school at fourteen, sometimes not taking up scholarships for further education because their families could not afford to keep them on at school. They then went into service, often in the same area, or increasingly worked in shops or offices until marriage. After marriage, many women needed to supplement a meagre family income and took part-time cleaning work in private homes and offices. Mrs. Margaret McLean, who was born in Bickerton Street in 1887, used to work five mornings a week for the French Consul in Ullet Road for 10/-, and paid 3/- to another woman for looking after her children during this time. On leaving school, boys would frequently take up their father's trade, find a job in business through personal recommendation, or join the Merchant Navy.

The greatest change seems to have come in the lives of middle-class women, who rebelled against lives of enforced idleness and insisted on being allowed to train for some kind of meaningful work. The surplus of single women because of the losses of the First World War reduced marriage prospects.

The women's suffrage movement, the development of girls' grammar schools, and the admission of women students to the University of Liverpool all helped to increase their expectations.

Often this brought conflict with their fathers, and several of the girls who lived around Lark Lane, including Miss Doris Forster and Dr. Grace Gillespie suffered mental breakdowns before gaining the freedom to lead their own lives. On the whole, this freedom was restricted to single women. Upon marriage, women were still expected to devote their time to voluntary work for the many local charities. Mrs. Elfreda Cotton writes:

> In 1922 I married Vere Egerton Cotton, and henceforth it was his interests which became mine, and I was fully occupied with them, and in addition with the Chairmanship of the Women Police Patrols, twelve in number, and with the Maternity Hospital. (Cotton, Reminiscences, p. 3. Typescript in LRO.)

Colonel Vere Egerton Cotton became a Conservative city councillor for the Aigburth ward in 1947, and Lord Mayor in 1951-52, presiding over the Festival of Britain events in the summer of 1951.

This period saw the introduction of private automobiles onto the Lane, although the old 'cabbies' were still much used. Motor cars would be driven occasionally down the Lane by private chauffeurs to allow their owners to do private shopping, although most orders from the big houses would be rung through and taken round by message boys and girls, either by bicycle or on foot.

The Park continued to be the focus of leisure activities in the area, and its attractions increased with the addition of an aviary, a copy of the Gilbert Scott statue of Anteros, a Jolly Roger pirate ship, and a Wendy Hut. But it was also competing with two new attractions: wireless, which had been introduced into school teaching from the late '20s, and cinema chains, which rapidly became a favourite haunt of courting couples.

During this period there are also signs of emigration from the area. Reduced prospects of employment and promotion in Liverpool drove the enterprising to try their luck elsewhere in the empire, although some men, such as Mr. Corkill, later returned to the Lane.

Whereas middle-class girls tended to be educated locally, many of their brothers were sent away to school, followed by university or further training. This often loosened their ties with the district. One pair who went away and then came back in retirement are Dr. Grace Gillespie, born in 1899, and her brother Mr. Bryce Gillespie, who was born in 1900. Grace was educated at the Belvedere School, studied medicine at Liverpool University and then worked for over twenty years at a medical mission hospital in Mysore, India. Her brother first attended a private school at 30 Parkfield Road, followed by boarding school in Cambridge. He then spent his working career as a teacher in New Zealand before returning to Lark Lane to retire. He and his sister now share their old family house on Parkfield Road.

Panorama of Central Liverpool showing war damage after the May 1-7, 1941 blitz.

Local elementary school Log Books of the late '20s present a sombre picture of regular outbreaks of influenza and diphtheria. Housing was often inadequate, and the combined family income of poorer families did not allow for adequate heating.

The End of the Big Houses, 1939-1959

War brought enormous changes to the area. Although no shops on the Lane itself were greatly damaged by bombing, the Blitz brought several direct hits in neighbouring roads. Mrs. Lulu Williams remembers sheltering in the reinforced basement in the electricity station during bomb attacks. Several of the big houses were requisitioned for military or hospital use, and most of the older merchant families moved out over the years. Mrs. de Larrinaga was one of those who remained.

Sefton Park suffered during the war. In August 1940, the Daily Post reported that the railings around Sefton Park had been 'taken down for Ministry of Supply purposes and were expected to yield about 140 tons of metal'. The glass of the Palm House was also smashed during the Blitz, and the plants perished. By 1951 the re-glazing had been started, in 1953 the aviary was restocked and in 1957 the Palm House was finally reopened.

Sefton Park Palm House, opened 1896.

As women moved for the first time into factory work, the supply of domestic servants shrank greatly. At the end of the war many of these women, such as Miss Iva Jones, decided to stay on in factory work since wages were higher than in domestic work.

Many local schoolchildren were evacuated for long periods to country areas in Wales and Cheshire, which brought a further disruption of family life. Some women, such as Mrs. Lulu Williams, née Tonkiss, took over the running of family firms while their husbands or brothers were away on active service. Other women played an active part in the war effort by driving ambulances, fire-fighting, running canteens for armed services, or helping in voluntary organisations.

After the war, as the work of reconstruction started, planners pointed to the fine residential possibilities of the area. In February 1948, Sir Lancelot Keay, Liverpool City Architect and Director of Housing since 1925, urged in the *Daily Post*:

> As the leases fall in, the Corporation would have a unique opportunity of securing redevelopment of that fine district, providing suitable dwellings of the current standard and amenity, and thus encouraging to return nearer the center of the city some of those who, for one reason or another, had moved elsewhere.

The following week the *Echo* applauded this suggestion, and stressed again the need to keep a mixed population living within the inner areas of the city:

> From its inner sections Liverpool has long been allowing (indirectly forcing) its more professional and cultured classes to migrate. We don't want a city of nothing but artisans, though our artisans are second to none…Here is the first installment to stop the exodus and rebuild a city for all sorts of folk. That is real democracy.

A Council report on the development of the periphery of Sefton Park in December 1958 points out that ninety-nine of the original Victorian villas around Aigburth Drive, whose ground landlord was the Corporation, had now been put to various uses as University hostels, old people's homes, a nursery school, a nurses' home, and a Territorial Army headquarters. It estimated that there was a population of around 1,000 living in other villas which had been privately converted into flats, with a further 300 living in hostels and other institutions. One of these institutions, Aigburth House, opened in 1954 and accommodated 57 old people; many more such homes were to follow.

As well as converting existing property to new uses, the Council also embarked on a program of new group building. Over a 20-year period, plans were laid to build 1,120 new dwellings designed to accommodate 3,700 people. These included tower blocks such as Belem Towers, a disabled persons' hostel on Livingston Drive, and the Bloomfield Green site at the bottom of Linnet Lane, designed to provide 50 1-bedroom flats for the elderly.

The siting of all these institutions and the introduction of a large proportion of elderly people to the district was bound to alter the former social structure of the area. A further significant change in the '50s was the rapid expansion of the student population, in Liverpool, and elsewhere. In the early '50s there were only three student halls of residence, so that there was a large overspill into the bed-sits and small flats into which many of the big houses had now been divided.

This period thus marks the beginning of a continuing polarization of the district between a young and transient student population and an older, permanent population.

But the full impact of these post-war changes had not yet been realised in the '50s. In many shopkeepers' recollections, this period is still seen as one of a return to normality and relative prosperity. Stevenson's, Hogg's, Tonkiss's and Glendinning's all carried on as they had done for the past fifty years or more. Uniformed nannies were still seen occasionally wheeling high prams along the Lane, and Cunard passenger liners still sailed regularly down the Mersey.

Urban Decline and Renewal, 1960-1980

The last two decades have seen more changes on the Lane than in any previous period. There have been gains and losses. On the negative side, physical decline has continued, with shops standing vacant for long periods, and the mushrooming of antique shops and restaurants in the area has sometimes been resented by the older local inhabitants, who fear that the night life is beginning to take precedence over the daytime shopping needs of the permanent residents.

On the positive side, a new community spirit has developed and taken concrete form in the diverse activities fostered in and around the new Community Centre in the former Police Station. And major strides have been made in conservation since the whole district was declared one of Liverpool's conservation areas in November 1976. Housing associations have completed major renovations on many of the big houses, and teams working for the Rural Preservation Association have carried out imaginative schemes involving the laying of footpaths and the planting of waste areas with shrubs and grass.

The '60s began with an air of hopefulness. A City of Liverpool Interim Planning Policy statement of March 1965 spoke optimistically of rising national and local prosperity, even though it warned at the same time that some 200,000 new jobs would be needed in the area by 1981. In the middle and later '60s, the rapid rise to fame of the Beatles brought Liverpool a new national, even international, recognition as a 'swinging city' second only to London. Merseyside Arts Festivals were organised in 1962 and 1963 by a group of people which included local popular poets Adrian Henri, Brian Patten and Roger McGough. Liverpool culture was gaining new prominence, the new Roman Catholic cathedral was being built and work was speeding up on the Anglican cathedral, and on the football field, Liverpool and Everton were triumphant.

In the Lark Lane area, new building continued. In 1967, Parkside, a Day Care Centre for the physically and mentally disabled with a purpose-built hostel and workshop, was opened in Linnet Lane. The following year saw the opening at the bottom of Livingston Drive of the Joseph Gibbons Day Centre for pensioners, next door to a new child welfare and family planning clinic.

By the early '70s, this mood of confidence was on the wane. It was fairly clear by now that the promised 'Merseyside renaissance' would not take place. Although multi-national companies such as Ford at Halewood had provided new jobs in the area, smaller companies began to collapse and an average of 30,000 jobs per annum were lost throughout the 60s. Employment on the docks continued to decline sharply, and in the '70s unemployment on Merseyside was three times the national average. Between the mid '60s and the mid '70s about a quarter of jobs in the manufacturing sector disappeared. In 1967 Cunard passenger liners moved from Liverpool to Southampton.

In the early '70s road development schemes blocked off the direct exit of Lark Lane onto Aigburth Road and an underpass was built. This meant that the shops in the Lane lost most of the passing trade, and business declined sharply. Around the same time, centralization of police services in South Liverpool meant that the old Police Station was no longer needed, and the property was put up for letting. In the mid '60s, Christ Church also sold its two properties on the Lane, the former Schools building and the ornate Institute building on the opposite side of the street. The City Council also decided to go ahead with demolition of old terraced housing in Hesketh Street, and several of the old inhabitants were moved out to a new estate in Otterspool. Mrs. Jane Baxter describes how the fear of the bulldozer suddenly seized the district.

At this point, as Lark Lane seemed about to succumb to the blight of other inner-city areas and the old community looked on the brink of disintegration, various groups began to assemble in order to work out new methods of survival. The rest of this recent history is recorded in the information sheet of the St. Michael's and Lark Lane Community Association:

> In April 1975 a group of local inhabitants called a public meeting at the Albert Hotel in Lark Lane to discuss the formation of a Community Group for the St. Michael's Ward. By coincidence, another public meeting was called for the same evening in Linnet Lane to test support for a Community Association for the Lark Lane area.
>
> Both meetings were well attended, proving that the area badly needed a wide range of community activities and that there were a lot of people willing to do something about it.
>
> The meeting held in the Albert led to the formation of the St. Michael's and Lark Lane Community Group, which very rapidly expanded the activities of the junior football teams, initiated Sat-

urday morning swimming classes, and began a tote to pay for the new activities. Within its first year, the Community Group also ran a Youth Club in the hut on Dingle Field, ran some discos, and introduced Summer Play schemes to the St. Michael's area. Only the need for a permanent base restricted further expansion.

From the other public meeting emerged the Lark Lane Community Association, which fostered the Pre-School Playgroup and the Lark Lane Housing Co-op as well as pressing for local conservation areas and getting involved in local planning issues.

In 1976 the two groups decided to amalgamate into the St. Michael's and Lark Lane Community Association and to lease the former Police Station for use as a Community Centre. In November 1976 they moved in and immediately began extensive fundraising and renovation of the building. At the same time, the district was officially declared a Conservation Area and in 1978 the Community Centre was awarded a 5-year Urban Aid Grant.

Old Police Station, built in 1880s. Watercolour by Dave Turton.

Gradually, trade on the Lane began to pick up, new shopkeepers moved in, the wine bar and bookshop opened, and unpretentious antique shops opened to cater for the furnishing needs of the large student and singles population in the area. Sunday visitors to the Park began to explore the Lane, and an area that had recently looked about to collapse now showed many signs of new life. The old community and the new community were now trying to work out a future that could benefit them both.

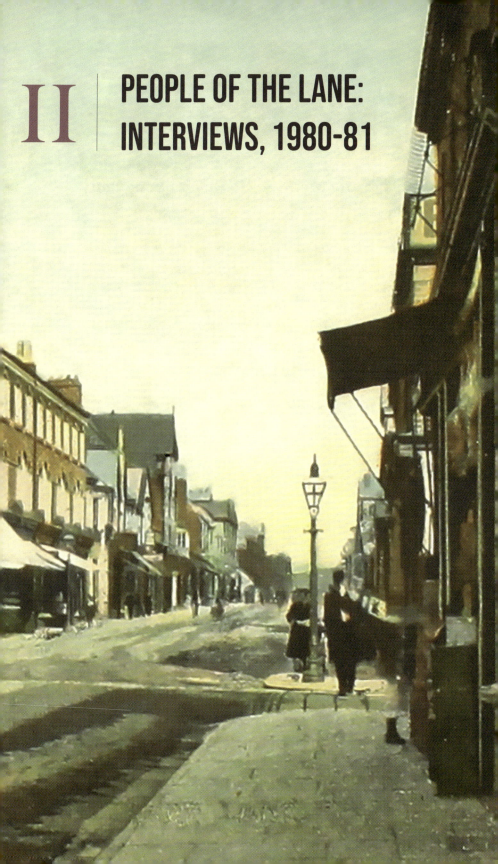

II | PEOPLE OF THE LANE: INTERVIEWS, 1980-81

II | INTERVIEWS: 1980-81

Mrs. Margaret McLean: 'It's Such a Long Story.'

A passionate Lark Laner and twice widowed, 'Aunty Maggie' is a community-minded person who brought up six children and worked in many jobs downtown and around the Lane. Her first job was in a local hat shop and involved walking all the way from Aigburth to North John Street and back. 'You had to either work or starve,' she says.

Margaret McLean. Photo by Tom Wood (hereafter TW).

My Father

I was born in 14 Bickerton Street in 1887. My name was Margaret Richardson. My father was a chimney sweep, he used to work in all the big houses. He got a shilling a chimney, but they never paid him while he was on the work. He had to buy what they called 'heads' with his name on, and I used to have to go around the houses and say to the maids 'Please, me father sent me for the money for the 'chimbleys.'

Bickerton Street.

We were poor, we had sugar butties for breakfast. There used to be a milk house down Lucerne Street, where you could go and get a pint of milk. It was tuppence for a 2lb. loaf. They would weigh it and if it was under put a jockey on the top, a scone or a piece of bread. We used to get one ounce of tea for a penny, nobody ever got more than two ounces at a time. Meat used to hang outside in Park Road, it's a lot cleaner now. The shops were open until midnight. You could get a leg of lamb for a shilling. I used to like curried corned beef.

A Lovely Pan of Scouse

In Lark Lane at the corner of Waverley Road there was the butcher, Mr. Lewis. The gentry used to have all their meat cut there, all trimmed up lovely. There'd be pieces of meat left on the block, and for threepence we could get three penn'orth of pieces to make a lovely pan of Scouse. You could buy a ha'porth of carrots and a ha'porth of onions, and five pounds of potatoes would cost about three ha'pence. Carrot, onion and meat. You know what, my father used to call them 'rough ornaments.' You'd cook the meat and the vegetables first, then cook the potatoes and put them in.

Memories of the Lane and the Park

It was lovely on a Sunday morning because the Salvation Army used to come in the Lane. There was a man who would call out 'Light cakes! Three a penny light cakes!' And someone else would say 'Sandbags for sixpence!' Every day there would be a barrel organ outside our door, mostly foreigners. My mother would give them a penny. I remember a woman with a box in front of her organ and she had a child in that box. My mother gave her a cup of tea, and she found that the child's feet were tied up tight in rags. Maybe they were Chinese. There was also a Russian with a big bear. He used to go around the Drive and make it stand on its hind legs, then the children would throw money down.

Sefton Park ice.

We children were always in the Park or on the Cast Iron Shore. My eldest brother Thomas had a boat, and he used to catch eels. We had lovely summers. You could depend on a summer.

In winter, Sefton Park lake used to be frozen for weeks at a time. People would go skating on it. My brother used to pay a ha'penny or a penny for a big empty orange box at the greengrocer. Then he'd buy a ha'porth of candles and take a chair, box and candles and sit at the side of the lake. The people would sit on the chair while the lads put their skates on them. And they would give them a copper for doing this. The reflection of the candle lights on the lake were really lovely.

Billy the Barber

The first house in Bickerton Street used to be a barber's shop. The parlour was a shop. We used to go to the lobby as kids and shout out 'Billy the barber, shaved his father with a rusty razor. The razor slipped and cut his lip, poor old Billy the barber!' There was a general shop next door. I worked there for a while. The husband had a hansom cab and used to wait at a stand on the corner of Lodge Lane and Ullet Road. Sitting there on the top. His wife ran the shop. She used to boil eggs, and all the boys used to come in. It was a ha'penny for a bottle of pop and a hard-boiled egg.

The Band of Hope

My mother never knew the taste of drink. There was an old woman who lived next door who liked a glass of beer before bed, and as a child I used to go to the Masonic and get a jug for her. Then I joined the Band of Hope, which had started holding meetings in the Lane. You weren't supposed to handle drink, have nothing to do with it. So I wrote a note to my neighbour: 'Dear Mrs. Smith, Sorry I can't go for your beer any more. I've joined the Band of Hope.'

Madam McKay

Norman Bros., had a board on the slant, and in gold letters it said 'Madam McKay'. One day it was there, and the next day gone. 'What have you done with Madam McKay?' we kept asking.

Early Jobs around the Lane

When I left school I went to work in Pelham Grove doing housework. Using the old irons. I think I got 1/6. The lady said to me ' You're a good little worker.'

I remember when I was looking for a job I was told they were having a party on the corner of Sandringham Drive. There was a cook, a waitress and a housemaid. I was supposed to carry the food into the dining room and place it on th e sideboard. But at the last minute I was too shy, and I ran away, came home!

I left school at fourteen and worked in a hat shop on the Lane. The ladies used to wear ostrich feathers. I used to take their feathers to a shop in North John Street, where they would curl them. I got 1/6 a week. I walked there and back, wearing button-up boots and black stockings. We used to wear lovely Leghorn hats, and I had a shot silk parasol. My mother made all our clothes. When my baby sister Rachel Alice died from measles at the age of three, I remember my mother made her a green velvet bonnet and coat.

Then I went into service at the top of Parkfield Road as a kitchen maid. We got out only once a week, from 3 until 9 o'clock. I was so keen to get out just for a little walk! I remember saying to the head waiter 'Can I go and post a letter?' when I hadn't really got a letter, just something scribbled on a piece of paper. Then he let me go out to the pillarbox opposite.

Where I Lived

It's such a long story when I look back. I was only little when I moved from 14 to number 1 Bickerton Street. That's where my father and mother died. Porters buried my father. My mother was 85 when she died, in 1939. She was still living in Bickerton Street.

I got married in 1907 when I was 20. My husband Alexander McLean was a cook on the Harrison boats, and he'd go away for about three months at a time. He wanted me to go and live down

Rear of Grafton Street.

near the docks, right by where the ships used to come in, off Grafton Street. We lived in Denison Street. Our six children were all born down there. Dockers wanted to live there because they had to go down twice a day in the hope of being picked. The pay was 4/- a day, if you worked.

I used to walk from Denison Street every morning up to the French consul general's house in Ullet Road. I worked there four mornings a week for seven years for 10/- a week. A woman came in to look after my children, and I paid her 3/- a week. I had a lovely reference after he left when he was posted to Germany. It was very hard work then, you didn't use mops, you had to get down on your hands and knees.

Men never did any work with the children. You never saw a man pushing a pram, and they never looked after the children at night. They would go out to the pub or some place, you would never ask them where they went.

You had to either work or starve. I'd buy the children's shoes second-hand down in Paddy's Market. I'd get up before 5 o'clock and take the tram down to clean offices in Dale Street. You had to be there from 6 until 9, to light fires and do the dusting. Then we had to go back again from 5 until 8 in the evening, doing the dirty work, doing the fires and scrubbing the floors. I was there for a couple of years.

Bad Day in Paddy's Market

Paddy's Market used to be in Scotland Road. When my husband first would join a ship, you had to take your marriage lines down to the offices to get your pay. So one morning I was on my way there and my reference and my marriage lines were in my bag. I went to get a pair of shoes for me son from Paddy's Market. We couldn't afford new shoes. I can still remember these young girls behind me. And all of a sudden my bag was gone! I had to send away to get a copy of my marriage lines.

The Sinking of S.S. Artist

During the First World War my husband was chief cook on the Harrison boat *S.S.Artist*. When I went down to the offices to get my pay in January 1917, I was told the ship had been torpedoed in terrible weather in the Irish Sea and was missing in the Channel. Two of the lifeboats had gone down with the ship! We had to just wait and wait for more news. Then I was told that my husband was one of the few survivors. Sixteen men were drifting in a lifeboat in icy waters for three days. Some were frozen stiff and were tipped overboard. They were only found because my husband's cook's apron was hoisted as an S.O.S. signal. He was taken to hospital in Ireland suffering from frostbite. He was never strong after that.

Widowed

My husband died in 1933 of tuberculosis. I was 46, with six children, three sons and three daughters. The three youngest were still at home. My youngest daughter was 8, one was 11 and the next was 14. There was only parish in them days. If you got any money from them, they'd come to your house. If you had anything like a radio, you had to get rid of it, or they wouldn't give you anything. As a widow I got 10/- for myself, 2/- for the 8 year old, and 3/- for the 11 year old. Nothing for the 14-year-old. I didn't know at the time about a seamen's fund called St. George's Fund, I only learnt about that later. I came back to live in number 3 Bickerton Street, opposite my mother. I was paying 6/- a week rent.

Back to Lark Lane

About 1941 I came back to Lark Lane from St. Michael's. They wanted someone to be a caretaker in Hargreaves Road, so I came here as that. 'All I want you to do are the stairs,' he said, 'and I will charge you 8/- a week rent.' I've been here 39 years. I've always loved housework. It was coke fires then.

I stopped working when I was over 70.

It's such a long story when you look back. I call them the good bad old days. We were slaves then. When there were no unions you just had to work or starve, but now unions do fight for them. My son is a member of the Boilermakers' Union. He's got that asbestos disease, because he had to work with blue asbestos.

My Harmonica

What I like to do now is play the harmonica. I taught myself, and about four years ago I was the winner in a competition for elderly people. I've played it at the Neptune Theatre, and hospitals as well as in the Community Centre. The old people know all the old songs, and they usually join in. My daughter wants me to go and live in Leasowe, but I said 'No, I was born in Lark Lane and I'll never leave it.'

WORKING ON THE LANE

1. Stevenson's Cake Shop

In 1980, several shops on the Lane still had their original names since opening in the second half of the 19th century. Stevenson's, the cake shop, opened in 1868. It was run for many years by the Misses Stevenson, and a great favourite with children.

Miss Joan Carey, born in 1902, recalled:

There were two delightful women in Stevenson's on the Lane. Mother used to take us shopping there, all three of us, all dressed alike. She made most of our clothes, I can remember we had red coats and red bonnets with ribbons. I was always dressed in dark clothes, and the other two wore lighter ones, because I was always dirty. I thought I ought to have been a boy. Only one of us was allowed into Stevenson's, because the Miss Stevensons gave a piece of fudge to the one who went in. And it was lovely! And so of course we had to wait for three weeks to get our turn for the piece of fudge.

Miss Doris Forster, born in 1893, recalled:

When we were children, during the week we had bread and butter with jam, no cake. But we went to Stevenson's every Saturday morning and were allowed to choose our own cake for Sunday. My favourite was slices with pink and white icing. They still have them.

Miss Edwards, cook, started working there in 1931:

I came in when I was fourteen, working for Miss Stevenson of Grassendale. I delivered orders and helped wash up in the back. You started that way. I was still living in the Dingle then. Later I moved out to the Lodge Lane area and since 1940 I've been living in Aigburth. I would go out with baskets delivering on foot, out to Mossley Hill and Greenbank, all over.

Then you sort of worked your way into the bakery part. We didn't bake bread, more batch cakes and bridge rolls. We used to make ice-cream too, and delivered that at seven o'clock at night ready to put on the table for dinner parties. We put them in moulds, and then in ice-buckets. I used to like the ice-cream with nuts in, and the one with fresh strawberries.

We also did decorated meringues, and big steak and kidney pies. Very little of our recipes have changed. And the ovens are the same. They were converted from coke to gas just before I started here in 1931.

Lark Lane used to be a good busy centre with lots of little general shops. The Old Police Station added to the life of the street, and I'm sorry that's gone. At the moment we seem to have a lot of antique shops and restaurants, it's not so good for shopping. And they should have thought of something different from the subway at the end. It's too much for older people of the likes of me, going up 20 odd steps with heavy shopping baskets.

I enjoy working here, but let's face it, these days it gets a worry, sales aren't good. It's a long day. I'm in the shop by half seven, and most days I don't get away until about half six. At my age I think I've done my bit.

2. Glendinning's. Fish and Poultry

This is still an open-fronted shop, where fish are displayed on big marble slabs. Mr. William (Bill) Carmichael is the owner and manager.

Mr. Carmichael:

The Glendinnings started in Lark Lane in 1876. My father came here in 1912 as manager. Mr. Glendinning died in 1931, and my father carried on for his widow until 1945, when I came back from the war and took over.

I was born in Kensington, but moved later to Edge Lane. Then from when I was eleven, we moved to Bowring Park, and have been there ever since.

I served my time as an electrical engineer, then war broke out. After the war I had such a long leave that I came here for a few

Mr. Carmichael

Paul Mooney: 'My Dad Brian (from the old gun shop) sometimes used to play cards with Billy the Fish [Mr. Carmichael] and his son Peter at dinner time in the '70s. I remember the smells of fish, the sawdust, the rabbits' feet, and can still hear Peter's infectious laugh.'

weeks to pass the time, and I've been here ever since. We used to have two shops, the other in Lodge Lane, but we closed that down in 1960.

Compared to what it was, this area has gone down completely. You get a lot of vandalism. In 1945 we had more orders again than what we've got now. We used to have eight lads, now there's only my son and myself in the shop, and my wife helps with the paper work. Closing off the bottom of the Lane was bad for trade here. Shops here are more expensive, but they survive because they're more convenient.

My own trade has declined a bit over the past five years, because of the frozen foods for one thing. They do say people eat more fish in the summer, but with people going away and so on, we're busier in the winter. This is a good position for me, because my main rounds are up here and in Childwall, and my nearest competition is down at Aigburth Vale.

I'm also an area manager for the pools. That takes nearly all Friday night, till about twelve o'clock. I've got about thirty collectors, and I collect the coupons and the money off them.

Glendinnings

3. Tonkiss. Florists

Mr. H.H. Tonkiss, the grandfather of the present owner, came from Gloucester and was head gardener for the Duke of Westminster on his Sutton estate. His son William ran vegetable and flower shops on the Lane from 1911, and William's two children, Harry and Louise (Lulu), both entered the family firm.

Mr. Harry Tonkiss. TW

Mr. Harry Tonkiss:

I went to St. Michael's for a start, and then to the Institute. When I finished school, I was put on a farm for twelve months. My father's idea was to make you stand on your own two feet.

I've been working here since I was sixteen. When I was away during WW2, my father and my sister Lulu carried on the business. All the windows in the shop were blown out as a result of the landmine in Linnet Lane.

Our business is much smaller than it was, and the glasshouses at the back are derelict because it's not worth doing the nursery side. After the war we used to do a lot of decoration work, especially for the ships, and that side's all gone too. Now we mainly have small orders.

The Lane was very low for a while, but I think it's coming up now.

Mrs. Mary-Ann Tonkiss with her granddaughter Bessie Robinson, née Tonkiss, b. 1906. Bessie was brought up by her grandmother, and later lived in the household of her Uncle Will. Bessie's memories of being sent to buy dripping, and her fear of getting lost while delivering flowers to the big houses, have been preserved by her granddaughter Jennifer Robinson.

4. Mrs. Louise (Lulu) Williams, née Tonkiss

Mrs. Williams: Early Years

I was born in 1913, over the present shop at 121 Lark Lane. The bottom shop, Number 26, was my grandfather's. He had been head gardener for the (2nd) duke of Westminster on the Great Sutton estate. My father went to day school in the Christ Church Schools. When my father and mother were courting, they got the shop by the old Institute, across from the Schools building.

I attended St. Michael's. I remember Mr. Scott and Mr. Ringrose, a charming man injured in the war, who used to limp a little bit. Nice-looking man too!

I left school at fourteen, and was taught the trade. My father was one of those who said, if you haven't done it yourself, you don't know if people are doing it right, so I had to learn everything.

If the ladies in the big houses were having a dinner party, we would go and do a bowl for them, but otherwise they would do them themselves. We used to go down to *Tatoi, to a Greek lady called Mrs. Pallis, in the second house in the Drive. They had a big Daimler car, which they used to garage opposite Sefton Grove. Penny in the Pound started in a room over that garage.

* Named after the Greek summer palace 16 miles from downtown Athens.

Flowers on the Cunard Liners

In the old days we would go down to the docks at about 8.30 in the morning to do the flowers on the tables for the Cunard liners. Other times we would decorate St. George's Hall, we had huge palms we would use for that, and we decorated the Cathedral when Lord Derby's daughter, Lady Priscilla Bullock, was married.

A Terrible Snow

My husband and I began courting in 1943. I used to do a lot of ballroom dancing, and there was a bit of a competition on at the Grafton Rooms. I'd entered with a fellow who lived out at Aintree, and we'd got through the first round. I was terribly thrilled. We were due to go out again on the Wednesday night, and I'd borrowed coupons here and there to get a new frock for this blooming dance. But then there was a terrible snow, and he rang up to say he wouldn't be able to get through, because the trams weren't running.

I was terribly annoyed, and as I came out of the shop I slipped on the step, just as this policeman was going past. He picked me up and said "I'm just finishing now; would you like to go to the pictures?" And I was so cross I said "Yes, I would!"

After our marriage we bought a new house down in St. Michael's, opposite the station, and we've stayed here ever since. It cost us £1750, and as a policeman you earned about £350 a year. But we loved it here, it was so convenient. And in the old days you could get a train from here running right through to Hull.

Left: Wedding of Officer Owen Spurgeon Williams and Mrs. Louise (Lulu) Williams, née Tonkiss. *Right:* Wedding of Harry Tonkiss at Christ Church, Linnet Lane.

Harry Tonkiss outside the fruit and vegetables shop at 121 Lark Lane.

Shopkeepers and Residents

Lark Lane used to be a real village. Starting at the top there was McLeans, the undertakers. Two brothers, William and Tommy. Tommy had a big strong build. They had the horses down at the bottom, big black roans, I remember. Tom McLean moved to Admiral Street, and I think he had a son, but William McLean stayed on. He had a son and a daughter, Gladys. I was at school with her. She comes to the church. She married a fellow called Sam Kennerley. He lived in Bickerton Street. There was a big family of them, all born there.

Originally Charletts only had taxis. On Tuesdays nearly everyone on the Drive went to the Philharmonic, and Charletts used to send the cars round. Then, because more people were getting cars, George Charlett was sent up to McLeans to learn how to do undertaking. Alec McLean and George were friends. McLeans moved to Southport and Porters moved in for a while, then transferred all their business to the Dingle, and Charletts took over all the undertaking.

Lark Laners used to be buried in Smithdown Road, and later Allerton, we didn't hear much about cremation in those days.

Who lived Where

At the corner of Livingston Drive lived the Warings, from Waring and Gillow. Then Sir Ernest Cain. Lark Lane was like a village. All the people used to come down in their cars.

On a Friday around half past nine, the Misses Hughes would be down. There were five sisters and one brother. They lived in 5 Linnet Lane. After the bomb dropped, they moved out to Heswall and gave the house to the Church. The bomb shifted a lot of the aristocrats out. There was the Winders, they lived in number 1, they moved over to Heswall. And the Cohans, when they came back they went to what is now the Hotel Alicia.

Flower shop of Mr. William Tonkiss at 65 Lark Lane.

5. Mrs. Edith Mary Barnard, née Osgood. Florist

Mrs. Barnard worked in the Lark Lane area all her life. She wanted to become a children's nurse, but her father insisted she had to learn a trade. Peter Vernon remembers Mr. Barnard wearing a flat cap and smoking a pipe. Interviewed in 6 Little Parkfield Road in 1980.

Mrs. Barnard:

My maternal grandfather was a ship's carpenter. He helped to build the Landing Stage. He used to take us down there when we were

Liverpool Landing Stage with luxury steamship *Lusitania*.

children and show us a plank that was in the wrong way, because they were drunk when they put it in. They used to get rum off the boats.

My mother was born in Bickerton Street. She went into service with the Rensburgs at 12 Ivanhoe Road, working as a house parlour maid. The Rensburgs were German Jews, merchant bankers, and they used to have all the musicians there. I remember Kreisler came once.

My mother first started by helping the cook. Then Mrs. Rensburg sent her somewhere to learn how to make pastry. You got jobs by recommendation. Once you had become known as a good worker to these big families, you never moved. But you didn't get a pension at the end of it.

My father Sidney Osgood, was in the Royal Army Ordnance Corps. He was a Kent man. There were 26 in his family. They lived at Chatham, and he lost eight brothers in one naval disaster. After that a rule came out that not more than two brothers could serve on any one ship.

After leaving the army, Dad came up to Liverpool and got a job in the Post Office. They moved first into a house in Bickerton Street and then into Little Parkfield Road, where I still live. There were three boys, and I was the only girl.

The No. 33 Tram

All of us worked in the area. An uncle used to drive the old No. 33 tram from Garston along Belvidere Road. My elder brother used to take milk out for Hogg's Dairy. When he got to the age to go out to work, he started at a grocer's on the Aigburth Road. So, then my dad said 'Right. It's your turn now,' and I was sent in to Hogg's.

Then when I was fourteen Mr. Tonkiss the florist said to me one day 'How would you like to be a flower girl?' And I said 'No thank you.' I'd always wanted to be a children's nurse. But he said 'You go home and ask your mother. Doesn't she think you'd be better taking a trade?' My mother said 'Oh, it's a wonderful business. I've known Mr. Tonkiss since he was this big. I said 'No, I want to be a children's nurse.' Then my father said 'Well, you're not leaving home to go and train as one. You go on up to the flower shop, and if you're of the same opinion when you're the right age for it then we'll think about it.' You see, you needed to wait until you were eighteen before you started training. So, I never did.

I started work at the flower shop at about 6/- a week. It was hard work, and Mr. T. was a harsh man, he used to say 'I'm the boss.' He said 'If you leave here, you'll never get another job like this.' Well, I left him on the Saturday and on the Monday, I started straight away at another florist's, Elsie Bruce in Renshaw Street.

In my experience of being with both classes, people who had been born to money like Lady Waring treated you as an equal. I always remember Mrs. Tonkiss saying to me, 'Whatever you do, NEVER deliver flowers to a tradesmen's entrance. Flowers go in through the front door.'

And, I can't remember who it was, I took her flowers one day and she said 'Get around to the tradesmen's entrance. Don't dare come to the front door with flowers!' So, Mrs. Tonkiss rang her up and said to her 'If you were a lady, you would know better!'

I don't think she gave us any more orders.

6. Charlett's (Funeral Services) Ltd

For many years Mr. Tony Hutchinson worked for Charlett's on Lark Lane, before moving to their branch in Park Road.

Mr. Tony Hutchinson, 1980:

I began working in the funeral business at the age of fourteen as an errand boy, and I've been at it now for forty-five years. My wife and I offer a 24-hour service, and I reckon that around 80% of our customers are personally known to me. My job is to put the family at their ease. I tell them that the dead person would not have wished them to be grieving, and I cheer them up by telling them that survival is in the thoughts of the remaining family. Let's face it – there's no such thing as the afterlife – though I don't tell them that!

I loved Lark Lane in the old days. Mr. Charlett was a real gentleman, he lived in the White House next to the funeral premises. We were very friendly with the former owner of the Albert, a retired sergeant, and with the men at the Police Station. When I began to work, horses were still used, then Packards, and then Cadillacs. Now we use mainly Daimlers.

There were very few cremations until the beginning of the 1960s. Now it's cheaper, and I think it leaves the relatives feeling uplifted. A burial is more upsetting, leaving someone in the ground. Cremation charges are £281 with a hearse and one car, and extra cars are £20 each. A grave cost £118 for a plot plus incidental charges, and funeral costs come to £222. We average around eight deaths per day, but it goes up to around fifteen a day in February, that's the worst time for the old people.

I've had no unusual requests for burial except one, about twelve years ago. A man rang the doorbell at 1.30am, wanting me to arrange a burial for his cat. He had put it in the fridge, and wanted to order a special oak coffin. I sold him that, but he couldn't get permission for anywhere to bury it. In the end he went off to London with it, but he failed there too, and came back to Charlett's several days later with the animal still in the coffin in his car. So, I sent him off to the Little Sisters of the Assumption in Aigburth Road, and heard no more.

7. John Hogg and Sons. Dairy

Mr. John Hogg remembers in 1980:

This is the oldest dairy in Liverpool, we believe it was started by my great-grandfather John Hogg (1848-1922), in 1872. He was a shepherd, and he came to Liverpool from Yorkshire. Quite a lot of North Country people came down in that year.

He started off in the Dingle with £11 and bought one cow. He walked everywhere, and gradually built up a business. First, he built the shippon, or cowshed, in Lucerne Street, and then he built the Parkfield Dairy, which was quite a showpiece in those days.

Musician Sean McLaughlin with family outside John Hogg & Son Dairy. TW

Later he bought and ran Jericho Farm, which was where the Quakers originally farmed. We were the last to farm down there. Then it had around 50 acres of dairy and arable, but around 1900 it was twice or three times as large, and spread right over Aigburth Vale. Now it's playing fields, and there's a small corporation estate on the site of the old farm buildings.

My great-grandfather was also one of the founders of the idea of cow keepers. There used to be one practically on every corner. They kept their cows in sheds called shippons. There were 900 cow keepers in Liverpool alone, but there are none left now. In the summer the cows would be taken out to graze on the golf links or at the cricket club. We used to graze all our animals down at Jericho Farm in the summer, and bring all the best milkers up to Alwyn Street and Little Parkfield Road in the winter.

My father had five sons, and we all joined the family business after leaving school at fourteen or sixteen, whether we wanted to or not. But we enjoyed it, it was very varied, healthy work. Around the drives we used to deliver in half-gallon cans. We had thirty cows, and they averaged around three and a half gallons a day, producing around 110 gallons. If you needed a bit more, you'd buy it in from outside.

We had all kinds of cows, but mainly Shorthorns and Ayrshires. The Frisians in those days gave the quantity, but their quality was poor. Then later on before or during the war, we imported Holstein Frisians from Canada. One of my uncles instigated that, and their milk was very good.

The cow keepers started disappearing around 1960. The system collapsed largely because of labour difficulties – people didn't want to work those hours. It was seven days a week. You milked at five in the morning and at four in the afternoon, even on Christmas Day, and you didn't finish until seven in the evening.

At one time Lark Lane was more like a country village than a town street, full of high-class specialist shops. Glendinning's, the fishmonger and poulterers, always had lots of game birds hanging outside. Now the area has changed a good bit, but I think it's on the way up again. Cutting off the end of the Lane seems to have been a good idea, it seems to have helped create a village atmosphere.

8. Mr. E. Callister. Quality upholsterer

I was born in Edge Hill, one of six children. My father was more or less a labourer, he used to work on the roads. I was good at woodwork at school and when I was fourteen a friend of my mother's told me to go down to a firm in town where she knew there was a vacancy. I thought I was going to be a cabinetmaker, but when I got there, they said they wanted an apprentice upholsterer. So that's what I became. The apprenticeship took seven years.

I came here eighteen years ago. I knew the area was quite good. Someone who lived opposite Charlett's and made kneehole desks said to me 'It's a good little area if you're ever thinking of starting up on your own.' Only 5% of my work comes from the immediate neighbourhood, the rest is from customers I've known for years. I do a lot of old-fashioned upholstery; we specialise in high-class work at the top end of the bracket.

Quite a lot of work comes in from Heswall, from shops and private customers in Chester, and from the Isle of Man. Years ago we used to do a lot of Victorian chairs that went out to America, about a hundred a year, I think. Colemans used to pack for us.

Crafts like this are dying out in England now because it's so hard to get apprentices who are really interested. It can be a trying business, especially if the wooden frame is damaged and you're trying to match up old wood. But we always manage in the end.

I don't use the Lane much because I live in Liverpool 18 and I go home for lunch. Just the stationers across the street and the post office. I suppose I use the Albert once a year. But I know everybody. It's a friendly sort of place and quite a good student environment.

9. Mr. Harry Corkill. Garage owner

I was born in Tramway Road in 1909. My father was a Manx man and worked for the market gardens in Sefton Park. My mother was a farmer's daughter down in Derbyshire. There were four of us in the family, I had two sisters and a brother. We all went to St. Michael's, and then I went to the Technical School in the Dingle for the last two years.

I used to go to the cinema a lot, and see these cowboy pictures of people who took a shovel and pick and dug up gold nuggets. So, I emigrated. I tried to stow away twice, but I was caught. The first time I was caught at St. John's and put ashore at Quebec. The next time I was caught at Montreal. I was homesick, and there was no work in winter.

Then I emigrated to Canada in 1928. I could have gone to Egypt – I was undecided whether to go to Africa or Canada. I stayed there over three years. You had to have £5. Then you went farming for five dollars a month. I landed in Quebec, then went out to a place called Orangeville, about seventy miles by train. We did harvesting. Then I went on the railway, and worked in a timber camp. I worked on the lake boats from Montreal. Eventually I jumped boat and made my way round to San Francisco, where I had six weeks harvesting. Then I started to hitchhike from there to Montreal.

I got back to Liverpool around 1932 and started at the Post Office, where I worked on the telephones for eighteen years. And then I ran a garage round in Little Parkfield Road.

I remember all the old shops in the Lane. There was a woman who used to run a cobbler's shop, Ma Kilmer. She was a great musician, played the violin. Someone came into the shop once and gave her a pat on the back to congratulate her. She swallowed a mouthful of tacks and landed up in hospital.

The barber used to go away to sea. Then he decided to give that up and start his own business. A lot of seafaring men used to make their way up to his shop in Lark Lane. One of them was a sail maker. He sat on the barber's chair and turned it round and round, then fell flat on his back. Word got out that William the barber had cut Wally the sail maker's throat.

10. Mr. G. J. Williams. Chemist

Mr. Williams began a three-year apprenticeship at Pwhelli at the age of sixteen, followed by a two-year course at the Liverpool College of Pharmacy. He moved to the Lane twelve years ago, taking over the shop from a Mr. Perkins, who had been working there for 43 years. A chemist shop has been on the same site for around 70 years, he believes.

Mr. Williams:

In a small shop you get a good relationship. Lots of people still come and buy things like cough mixture. The recipes are changing all the time. Still, some of the old-fashioned remedies, you can't beat them.

I'm on the committee of the Lark Lane Traders. It's a thriving little place which has had a definite rejuvenescence in the last two or three years. Part of this is due to the antique shops and restaurants. The night life is a good thing. People come here eating at night and look down the Lane, then come shopping in the daytime, people who have never been here before. We had some lean years about three years ago when the underpass was built, because we lost all the passing trade. But now it's all come back.

I'm as happy as one can be with trade at the moment. You've got to remember it's hard times for everybody. There's more competition than there used to be, now that toothpaste, toiletries and aspirins and so on are sold in supermarkets and other shops. We've had to diversify into health foods, for instance.

I take a course for pharmacists every winter at Clatterbridge, and I try to keep up with specialist reading. Then there's a couple of hours paperwork a day. I enjoy life as a chemist, but it's exhausting. You're very tied down, supposed to be on the premises all the time. I find most satisfaction comes from meeting people, and I love dispensing.

Mr. G.J.Williams at work dispensing.

The Williams pharmacy on the corner of Lark Lane and Bickerton Street in 1978. Sharon Jackson: 'I fell off my bike when I was about six. I had cuts to my hands and knees and a great big gash on my nose. Mr. Williams wiped my hands and knees and nose with Dettol and gave me a glass of orange cordial in the back room of his shop. He was a lovely man.'

11. Mr. Robert John (Bob) Smyth. Furniture remover

I've lived at several addresses in the district, first in The Elms, then in Park Road, and later in Livingston Drive North. My father was originally Irish, came over when he was a young man and never went back. He was a horse cabbie. His stand was at the corner of Princes Road, this end next to the park. The cabbies all had special stands, like the taxi ranks now.

In the old days it was much quieter. I remember at one time they covered a huge stretch of Belvidere Road with peat to deaden the

Smyth's Removals. *From left:* Mick Burns, unknown, Mick Reid (aka Cider), Alf Stansbie. TW

noise for a sick person. My father used to go up that way with the cabs and horses. As boys, we used to get the job of taking the horses for exercise with no saddle or anything, just a bridle.

I remember this area well in the old days. There were wooden blocks along Aigburth Road, because the trams ran down here. In the middle of the Dingle there was always a policeman on point duty. Then the Dingle Picture drome was built on the corner, with advertising hoardings around it. I saw my first cinematograph there, with Mary Pickford. Now of course it's turned over to bingo.

My mother was a splendid woman. During the First World War she was a Red Cross nurse, then she took up midwifery and practiced from Park Road, the family home, as a certified midwife. A very well-liked lady, very conscientious. We used to come home every day from St. Michael's for our dinners. Midwifery was the sort of business where you were called out night times rather than during the day, so I never remember any problems.

Nurse Rose Smyth

Bob Smyth with his mother. Photos courtesy of John Smyth.

I served practically all my time as a motor mechanic at Rushton's in Lark Lane. Mr. Rushton used to work at the Forge Cottages, and he was a very good mechanic. He had the cream round there: Rolls Royce's, Daimlers, Talbots. All the big houses round the Park were his customers, all chauffeur-driven cars, we were working on top class stock. I finished my time and left him before he moved up to the shop at the end.

These cars used to come down to the various shops – to Tonkiss's, then Glendinning's, all top-class shops. It seemed to go that way all down the Lane. The chauffeur would open the door and they'd go in and give their orders. Big families like the Molyneux-Cohans of Aigburth Drive. Even at that time they had five cars. Another very popular shop was Crews, the leather shop. They used to make and repair the leather for saddles, dog collars, and so on.

I set up the firm in the 1930s with my brother. Our first van was a model T Ford. We've found furniture removal one of the most interesting professions to be in. One week we were at Buckingham Palace delivering Princess Anne's wedding presents. The next week we were at Dartmoor Prison delivering a prison officer's furniture. Through the years we've come across most unusual jobs for what you might call a small-town firm. After the bombing of the House of Commons, the rebuilding and the refurbishing, it was this firm that delivered the new furniture. At the time we were contractors to the house of Waring and Gillow. They had a big factory in Lancaster, and the new furniture for the House of Commons was made there.

We meet every conceivable type of person. Sometimes there are sad cases of old people who are relying on you to help them but you daren't, because we have a moral obligation to keep the vans clean.

The job has changed a lot over the last twenty years. At one time we were protected by General Transport, no newcomer could come in and steal your business. Now we have to specialise in work that nobody else can do. We've got to the stage where we're the leading safe removers of this area. We've got the lifting gear for handling heavy safes up to four ton, putting them into offices and banks. Sometimes when a heavy safe won't go through the door we've had to take the wall down and build it all up again afterwards. We have a staff of 20 at the moment. We were operating ten vans at the start of the recession, now we've cut down to six.

I subscribe to the *Reader's Digest*, and I read the *Daily Mail* and the *Sunday Express*. My favourite recreation is modern sequence dancing. You have to learn the steps. It's very pleasant because you meet people of your own age. And you're not stuck with one routine, there are new dances coming up all the time.

12. Mr. C. E. (Charlie) Sexton of Hadassah Grove

Mr. Sexton moved to Hadassah Grove in the early 1950s. He earned the nickname 'The Guardian of the Grove' because of his efforts to preserve the private character of the Grove, which is an unadopted area.

Mr. Sexton:

I've lived in this house for a little over 30 years, since the early '50s. You can see the field boundaries of this area on an old map of 1769. This part of Toxteth Park only came into the Corporation at the end of the 19th century. I have a block plan of Hadassah Grove dating around 1890. Originally there were four gateposts, two at each end, which were closed at 10pm every night and unlocked by a gatekeeper. In the late 19th century there was a woman called Isabelle Strange, whose family owned number 1 and 19. She locked the gates each night at 10pm. But she died in 1901. The iron gates themselves went during the war, and no-one else took on running the Grove until I came.

Aigburth View obviously had a good view back then. Hesketh Street was named after William Hesketh, who was Vicar of

Hadassah Grove. Houses date from the 1840s.

St. Michael's for almost 35 years. And Lucerne Street probably referred to fields of lucerne. The shops spread out from Hadassah Grove, which at one time had a shop and a pub. Down at the bottom was an area known as The Old People's Plantation.

I was born in Fulham. It's fashionable now, but it wasn't then. My parents never got on very well with one another, or with me. My father had his right arm broken when he was nine years old. It was set wrongly in a fixed position. He had a pretty rough time. He earned a few pounds by washing cars in a garage in Chelsea at night. I was the only child. My mother was always in service as a cook general. She'd live in, in those days you didn't have much choice. I had to light the fires and scrub the floors. I was mainly brought up by my father's mother, my uncle Charlie and my granddad. They meant more to me than ever my parents did.

I went into the building trade, then in the army. When I came out in 1944 the flying bombs were still landing. I thought I'd had enough bang bangs to last me all my life. I fancied Liverpool from what I'd seen in the army, so I came up here and got a job in the hair and feather works. That was where I met my wife. She is a Liverpudlian and lived in Upper Mount Street. There were three sisters and four brothers in a double house, which is demolished now.

Around 1951 I started up independently in the building trade. Another builder moved here at the same time, and he helped me. I've never advertised, I do it all by personal recommendation. Then it was mainly small repair work, roof work. These days I do larger jobs because most people are using grants. So, I have to do a pretty comprehensive job with plumbing, rewiring and so on. My son now works with me and does most of the plumbing. There are an awful lot of cowboys about.

I still have some very old-fashioned views. I wish there were still more upper classes around, I think we can afford them. I don't care what sort of society you're in, you've still got the nobs up there, and they still lord it over you. One way and another, I don't think it matters. The real gentry never looked down their nose at you. I was working once in Sefton Drive and knew the lady there very well. I went once to the front door and the servant told me to go around to the side door. But Mrs. Davison (they had large landholdings in Derbyshire), just said 'Come in, come in, Mr. Sexton.'

13. Mr. Jim Duffy. Butcher - 1980

Mr. Duffy is always joking with older customers in his shop at 41 Lark Lane, which has the traditional sawdust floor, heavy marble table tops and wooden chopping blocks. Meat deliveries are made by van from the Stanley Abattoirs.

Mr. Duffy:

I took over the shop here in Lark Lane 24 years ago. The previous man was emigrating. Before that I'd been a butcher's manager at a

Jim Duffy. Paul Banks: 'This photo brings back so many nice memories. The saw, the hooks, the cellophane wrap and even the paper, which we used to cut to size. Collar and tie always.' TW

shop in Lodge Lane. I went into the butcher trade straight from school. My family comes from Anfield. My father went to sea, then worked for the electrical supply.

I suppose I know just about everyone on the Lane. The blocking off of the end of the Lane was bad for trade for a while, but it's picked up again now. But we need a supermarket, and more food shops. It would also be good to have a man's shop and a woman's shop. There's not much you can buy in the way of shirts or shoes. All these new antique shops and cafes are good for the night life but not for day trade.

Paul Banks:

My brother Stephen, my dad and I all worked for Jim Duffy at some point. My dad was manager of the Co-op butchers on Aigburth Vale before he got a job on the docks (dockers were still casual workers then). He helped Jim Duffy out near Christmas and at weekends. I first worked for Jim Duffy as an order boy/shop lad from age 13 to 18, when I joined the RAF. That was in 1970. Stephen went on to serve his time as a butcher with Dewhursts, becoming their youngest shop manager. He went on to buy Jim Duffy's old shop and became well known on the Lane.

I learnt to ride a bike on my 13th birthday. The following week I joined Jim Duffy on a week's trial. He asked me to sweep up, and make sure I got the brush under the counter. Then he went off to the loo. I found a fiver in the sawdust under the counter, so I cleaned it and put it on the counter. Jim came back and I told him I'd found the money. "Good lad" he said. It was undoubtedly a test.

I used to pick and buy all his wife's Christmas, birthday and Valentine's cards from Mr. Shabaily's. So many great memories of Jim Duffy! He was in the RAF during the war in the far east on RAF motor boats. He was captured and was a prisoner in a Japanese POW camp. He had some terrible stories of the abuses meted out. The other prisoners called him 'One Round Duffy', he told me, because he soon realised that if the guards hit you and you got up, then they would hit you again. Sensible man!

Ann White:

My mum always sent me to Mr. Duffy's on Saturday for a leg of lamb. Tuesday it would be braising steak, and Scouse on Wednesday. Thursday it would be Scouse pie from Wednesday's left-overs.

Bob White:

My mum would buy a pig's head, and ask Mr. Duffy to leave the eyes in, as it had to see us through the week!

14. The Sunshine Café

This small café at the top of the Lane is open from 8am until 2:30pm. It is well-patronised by the local people and run by Mrs. Parry. Radio 1 plays all day.

Mrs. Parry:

This place has been run as a café since about 1948. It didn't have a name when we came. We rent it, and registered it as the Sunshine Café about two years ago. An old man told me that when it first opened it was an olde-world sort of café with little tables and tablecloths, and the manageress wouldn't let any workmen in, then later it was turned into a milk bar, so I was told.

Our main competition on the Lane are the two chippies and Keith's Wine Bar. We do quite a lot of carry out food. The garages all come in here, it's mostly the people around Lark Lane who come. I do most of the cooking.

I hadn't any catering experience except at home. When I left school, I worked as a fur machinist. Then I went to work at Ford's as a sewing machinist. As my children grew up, I wanted something to do and thought I'd like to have a go at this sort of thing. And it wasn't too big a place, just what I wanted really. It seats about 21.

I thought it was just ample for me to be able to manage until my children have left school – after that, I don't know.

I love it here, meeting people and getting out of the house. I wouldn't go back to factory work now. This is more interesting, you meet different people every day, and it's varied. Some days we're really busy and other days it's dead slack. We stick mainly to what the lady used to do before. And we make all our own scones and our own pies.

We used to have one old lady come in up to a couple of weeks ago. She was 92. We get mainly workmen, but also a few ladies. We go across the road to the newsagent every day to get the Echo, and I do other shopping here too. I've grown to like the Lane very much.

Mrs. Parry and co-worker, Sunshine Café. TW

15. Turn of the Century. Antique Shop

The owner, Mr. E. Low. bought the shop in 1972 and opened for business at the end of 1975. He also plans to open a Mexican restaurant at the top of the Lane.

Mr. Low:

This is a good area for any unusual kind of business. When the end of the Lane was blocked off the area lost passing trade and a new

Couple outside Turn of the Century. TW

wave of different kind of businesses started moving in. I think I was the first of the new antique dealers. But Martins, on the site of what is now the French restaurant, had a well-established antique business. They used to get lots of people bringing them in stuff and calling them out to their homes because they were well known in the area.

I come from Southport, and my professional qualifications are in social work. I was always interested in psychology and did an 'O' level in it. I had planned to go on to university and study it, but instead I left school and went into psychiatric nursing. At first I found it totally shattering, but then I became fascinated by the study of abnormal behaviour and got first a psychiatric and then a general nursing qualification.

I spent about ten years in Australia, from 1963-72, did a course on teaching and taught nursing for a while in Adelaide. I also had a couple of antique shops in areas similar to this, the old parts of Adelaide and Sydney that had retained all their character. Then I came back to Liverpool and worked for the social services for several years.

My main customers are the young professional couples who are moving back into the area. There are also a lot of students who come in and buy odd bits. Trade is the worst it's ever been. The people who buy up large lots for shipping off to America have almost stopped buying because of the recession and the unfavourable rate of exchange. But business on the Lane is generally on the increase. The wine bar and restaurants bring more people into the Lane, so do the antique shops. I feel very much part of the Lane now. I use it for shopping and I know everyone.

16. Mrs. Annie Beattie. Launderette

The Pelham Launderette is on the corner of Pelham Grove and Lark Lane, opposite the Albert Hotel and Keith's Wine Bar. Mrs. Beattie knows everyone on the Lane.

Mrs. Beattie:

I've been in Liverpool for twelve years, came here to join my brother. I live on my pension with my daughter. She's a nurse, so I want for nothing.

Mrs. Annie Beattie in the launderette. TW. Granddaughter Debbie Fairfield: 'Nan was such a strong and beautiful woman, we all miss her still.'

I was born in the East End of London, just around the corner from the Mint in Whitechapel. My father worked on the horses and carts for a firm that got taken over by Pickfords. They were hard times. There were eight of us, seven brothers and me. I went to Tower Hill School when I was three. It was very strict, we used to get such clouts round the face for nothing at all really, not opening the door for a teacher, things like that.

Annie aged 21.

When I left school at fourteen, I worked for a while in a box-making place for 8 shillings a week. I had to give it all to my mother, and you'd get maybe sixpence back.

Then my mother died. She was only 43, quite a young woman. Died of galloping consumption. I remember going into the hospital to see her at the last. I had my little brother with me. I had to take him everywhere. 'Take him home,' she said. 'I can't be bothered.' I stayed at home from then on, but I was ignorant. I'd never learned anything about cooking. One of my brothers would come home for his dinner, and I'd have maybe just a plate of rice for him.

Later I worked as a waitress at the ABC in Oxford Street. I got eight shillings a week and then tips on top of that.

I got married when I was 24. My husband used to go away to sea. When the last war was about to break out, he joined the army. I moved up to Dundee in Scotland with our child, that's where my husband came from. He was brought out of the army with some complaint, and we had seven more kiddies. But then he ran away to London with a girl, and I had to bring them up myself. Our oldest was fourteen, the youngest a year and ten months. I went out to work in a tearoom and my oldest girl looked after the younger ones.

I've been coming in here for eleven years, but it's not really a job. I don't get a wage, nothing like that, just a couple of odd pounds.

I wash the towels for Keith, and he sends cups of tea over. It's just opening and closing the shop really, and I can go out when I like.

A lot of our old customers used to live in Hesketh Street and Bickerton Street, the side they pulled down. We don't get as many customers as the launderette down on the Aigburth Road, we close early for a start. But you don't get so good a wash down there!

My life is much easier now than when I was younger. I go twice a week to bingo and spend about £2.50 I suppose. There's quite a few of us all go together, they keep a table for us.

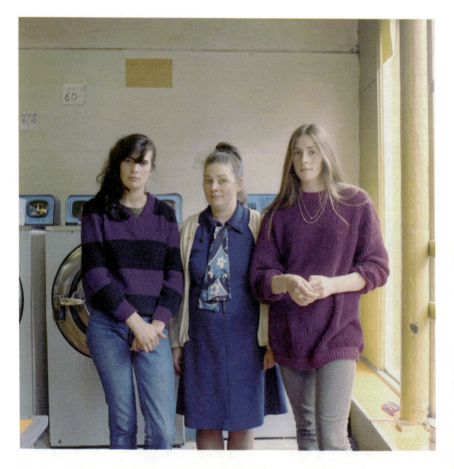

Mother and daughters. From left: Sue Oates, Mrs. Kathy Oates, Sandy Oates. Mrs. Oates, who lived next door with her large family, worked alongside Mrs. Beattie for many years, making the launderette a virtual children's playground and a great community hub. TW

17. Lesley Phillips. Bookshop

Whereas the library at the bottom of the Lane tends to be used more by the older inhabitants, the bookshop at the top caters mainly for the young bed-sit population and children. It is run by Lesley Phillips and her husband.

Lesley:

I'd been working before in Wilson's paperback department in Renshaw Street, and then I moved to this area and felt that this site would be perfect for a bookshop. We opened up around 18 months ago. There was another bookshop here for a short time before that, and earlier still it was an electrician's.

We offer good quality fiction, political pamphlets, feminist literature, and children's books and comics. Also, American comics such as Heavy Metal and Savage Sword of Conan. Most readers of these are in the 20-30 age group, some are a bit younger. Other popular sellers at present are Fay Weldon and Vera Brittain.

Our readership is the student and the academic floating population in bed-sit land in this area. We find it useful to be open all day on Sunday, because that's the only time a lot of them have just for browsing. I wouldn't say that the shop is used much by the working-class population, apart from the children's section, where you regularly find mothers buying books for their children.

I like the Lane very much, but I hope that the development of the night life doesn't squeeze out the other shops. Before Keith's opened, I think there were only two chippies and a Chinese restaurant. We need a good grocer. I'm very sorry that the Sugar and Spice run by Mr. Stewart closed down.

Pip Schofield comments in 2019:

This photograph of me by Tom Wood was taken outside Lark Lane Books on the corner of Sefton Grove, opposite the Old Police Station, the home of St. Michael's and Lark Lane Community Centre (SMLLCA). At this time, I was working as a Research Fellow for a PhD, studying the chemotherapy of malaria at Liverpool School of Tropical Medicine.

Above this shop, on the second floor, was the flat of my future partner Shirley St. Clair. Shirley was a chef in Keith's Wine Bar from the day it opened in 1979. The flat always had a roaring fire in the

Pip Schofield in front of the Bookshop. TW

winter, and you looked out through a corner turret to see everything that happened on Lark Lane.

Shirley commandeered a room on the first floor and turned it into a vintage clothes and antiques shop. It finally closed after Thomas the puppy dog, having been left alone in the shop for a few hours, ripped all the clothes to pieces. (He was especially fond of the fur coats).

The Community Centre as Catalyst

The community centre was a crucible (catalyst), for a number of projects, including the founding of the "Rural Preservation Society (RPA)", which eventually became the Landlife International Wild

Shirley St. Clair, girlfriend and later wife of Pip Schofield. TW

Flower Trust with its centre in Bowring Park. This was directed for many years by another local, Grant Luscombe, who now lives in St Michael's and received the OBE for his work.

The RPA built the first wildflower nature gardens in the country, along with Kevin Chambers from Manchester, at the International Garden Festival, Liverpool '84. They received three RHS gold medals. I was happy to be involved with the building of the gardens. My friend Dave Cornick, the tree surgeon (Dave the Tree), and I, cut down an old willow tree into stumps and planted them in the Nature Garden Lake, where they quickly rooted and grew into large trees.

I later managed the Nature Gardens for a number of years as they passed through different ownerships, and curated a 'Nature in the City' exhibition at the site. Sheila Large, my current partner and my wife, was the International Events Manager at the festival, and employed numerous people from in and around Lark Lane, including Terry Duffy, who is well known on the Lane.

Film Club

At the time of the photo, Maggie McCullough and I were running an art-style film club in the Old Police Station, known affectionately as "The Screen on the Park". We showed such classics as "The Creature from the Black Lagoon", when the audience wore special glasses to watch an early form of 3D. Shirley worked as the usherette selling ice cream and sweets from a tray around her neck. The 35mm celluloid films were rented from Top Rank and other Companies and delivered in tin film cans by Securicor.

Other Performances on the Lane

I was also involved and sang in a comedy performance style band called "Les Poissons D'Avril", (April fools in French), and we organised a number of family events at the Police Station including a Halloween Night and Seaside Rock. Our debut event was at the opening night of L'Alouette French restaurant on the corner of Lark Lane. I sang 'Under the Bridges of Paris' partly in French, and 'Matelot', a Noel Coward song. L'Alouette restaurant was run by Arthur, Vivien, Mike and Beatrice. Arthur Wilson later had successful delicatessen shops in Aigburth Vale and Bold Street, and now lives in the district.

The Sixties Revival Disco

One of my more infamous events at the Old Police Station was a "Sixties revival disco" run by myself and my friend Paul Russell, who later became a social worker. Paul had a huge collection of

13-15 Mannering Road. TW

Tamla Motown Soul and other vinyl single records, having been a DJ in the sixties. We scrounged some bamboo poles from a carpet warehouse in Chinatown and built a makeshift bird cage for the "GO GO" dancers. I was friends with Frank Clarke, Margi Clark's brother, who later directed the well-known Liverpool film *'Letter to Brezhnev'*. At the time he was keen to get an equity card to get into acting. We gave Frank a contract as a "GO GO" dancer to help build up his performance hours and get the card. On the night of the event, he arrived with an actress from *Brookside*. They came on stage to the Batman theme - Frank naked apart from a blue leather jockstrap. The actress was also topless. They danced very well. It went down a storm, but there was another storm the following week as I was hauled over the coals by the Executive Committee for putting on what they called a 'live sex show'.

Living around the Lane

At the time of Tom's photograph, I lived in a flat at 13 Mannering Road. Later, Shirley and I lived in Errol Street off Aigburth Road, with our children, Roisin, Alice, Lily and Joe. Once Sheila and I got together in 2001, we lived in the house called 'Glebelands', which was the first vicarage of St. Michael-in-the-Hamlet, the cast iron church.

18. Butterfield's. Fruiterer and Greengrocer

This is one of the busiest shops on the Lane. Mrs. Pauline Butterfield combines running the shop with bringing up her family of three children.

Mrs. Butterfield:

My father went away to sea. He was with Cunard, and moved down to Southampton when I was about eighteen. I was born in Wallasey and lived there for several years. My mother died when I was seven, and my grandmother brought me up from then on. I went to Liverpool Girls' College, and then worked for the Royal Insurance for two years until I got married.

Then my eldest son came along about fourteen months later, so I packed up work. My ex-husband used to work for his father's firm, which ran newsagent shops. He decided it was time to go on his own, and this was about the easiest job to go into because it didn't need a lot of capital to start off. We took a shop in Breck Road, and just went on from there.

We moved to the Lane in 1970. There was demolition going on behind the shop in West Derby, and the trade went down. Then this shop came up. The people here before were retiring. There used to be very old-fashioned potato bins, big copper things. It was dreadfully difficult to work in, so we had the shop completely refitted eight or nine years ago.

It's a bedsit community around here, and you get asked for a lot of things we never sold in West Derby, like garlic and ginger root. And lots of aubergines and courgettes. I think the area has declined from when we first came. The underpass knocked off a lot of passing trade. A lot of people don't even know Lark Lane exists.

The trade is quite good at present. I have a part-time assistant on Thursday afternoon and all day Friday, and two girls on a Saturday. I don't go to the market myself, I pick up a dealer who calls round three days a week.

Ideally, I would like to work part-time, but I'm on my own now, so I've just got to make the best of a bad job. But I can't just sit around either. I had six months off last year, and I couldn't wait to get back. I missed the people. I suppose I enjoy the work really. It's very long hours in the shop though, and then there's also the books to do.

They're working hard at developing a sense of community in the Lane. And the Community Centre is doing a very good job, trying to involve the children. I don't have much spare time with three children to look after and housework to do. But I do read a lot.

I get the *Post* and the *Daily Mirror* for the crossword. A friend passes on light reading to me, magazines and biographies, and books by Catherine Cookson.

I've moved a lot and I think I could live just about anywhere. It's a lot cleaner down in the south, but I like Liverpool.

Mrs. Pauline Butterfield, c. 2019.

19. Paul Robinson. Hairdresser

Contrasting styles are found at Paul's, still with its striped barber's pole, and at Barry Hayden's fashion-conscious salon.

Paul Robinson:

I started hairdressing when I was fourteen and lived in Gateacre. Then I emigrated to Australia for two years, worked in anything for a complete change and travelled all over the country. After that I decided to come back to England.

Paul Robinson in the doorway. TW

I've been on the Lane for fourteen years, and the first few years were difficult. In this trade, business is changing all the time. Long hair is in for a few years, then short hair. My customers are a lot of pensioners and some students, quite varied really. All the trade is regular, and my nearest competition is down on the Aigburth Road.

I love the atmosphere of the Lane. It has a village atmosphere. Everyone is very close and you get personal service. There are not many parts of Liverpool like this, the Lane is special. I go twice a week to the Albert or the Masonic. I play pool at the Albert, but I also know a lot of friends at the Masonic. That is a younger pub, whereas the Albert is for the older type of person.

I've also met my fiancée on the Lane; she works at Tonkiss's. Hairdressing is a good job for me because I enjoy meeting people. As soon as they walk in and sit down you can tell if they want to talk, and then you just encourage them. You get to know the regular customers very well.

Paul Robinson Interior. TW

20. Barry Hayden. Hairdresser

Barry Hayden:

I've been here three years now. The pensioners go mainly to Paul, and the people who come in here are mainly younger, say late 20s through 30-40. We do mainly modern work, but we also do lots of children.

At Barry Hayden's. Lynn Bligh McCann: 'This is my mate Linda Brett. She lived in Larkfield Road, but spent most of the time on the Lane with me. I lived at 119 Lark Lane.' TW

After leaving school I went straight into an apprenticeship in hairdressing. I used to work part-time in a pub in the evenings, because I was very poorly paid. I worked at various salons in town, and then opened up on my own about a year after being out of my apprenticeship. I've now got another salon out at Allerton.

Before moving here I'd been up and down the Lane looking for a shop and there was nothing available. Then a couple of weeks later this came up and I really begged the owner for it.

You've got absolutely everything here, including organ-builders and upholsterers. There are not many parts of Liverpool you can go now where all the little shops are still open.

21. Keith's Wine Bar

Since its opening in June 1978, this wine bar has become one of the best-known spots on the Lane. Open 7 days a week from 11 am until 11 pm, its simple furnishings and good range of wines and home-made food lend it an air of informality which blends in easily with the rest of the Lane. The owner, Keith Haggis, feels that his experiment has proved a success:

Keith Haggis:

After leaving school I started to study English at university, but then decided that architecture was the thing to do. So, I began another degree course, but instead of completing that I began working as a labourer for a building firm and stayed there for about 9 months. I had picked up a certain amount of theory from the architectural course, and practice from working with different trades, and my next step was to work on renovating a cottage in Wales for a friend. I spent about three months doing that, followed by a similar job for somebody else. It was at that point that this shop came up, and it just went on from there.

I'd lived around here for about four years, and it seemed to me that a wine bar was what was missing on the Lane. When we took it over there was only the front room being used as a shop, and that was in a bit of a state. Beyond that was only a storeroom and a backyard. We bought the property in December 1976 and from then until it opened in 1978, I was working on it, doing it up.

We're open pretty long hours. The first people in are the cleaners, between 8 and 9 in the morning. The girls start cooking about half 9, sometimes earlier. The bar opens at 11, and we're open right through until 11 o'clock at night, seven days a week. By the time you start clearing up at 11, you're not ready to leave until midnight at the earliest. Originally, I had to do the marketing as well, but we now have the vegetables delivered. I phone the order in and they're delivered twice a week. But I go myself to the meat market, to the fish market, and to the Cash and Carry. There's an infinite number

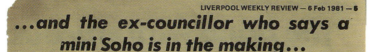

'Sin Lane'
Liverpool Weekly Review,
6 Feb 1981

of little jobs which have to be done, as well as buying the wine and keeping the books. My brother, who works with a firm of local solicitors, does every other weekend, so I get one weekend in two off.

A wine bar is a totally different thing from a restaurant, more like a café pub. You don't have to eat, and you can stay for hours or just for a quick visit. I've never been in a London wine bar, in fact I've only been in four other wine bars I think, and they've all seemed to have pretty different atmospheres.

Most of my customers are probably students or young professionals, along with other locals, but over the holidays when the students

Waitresses at Keith's, enjoying a break in Sefton Park. TW

are away, we still seem to be pretty busy. We also get people coming out from town for lunch, but not in a large number.

I live upstairs above the wine bar, and I use the Lane all the time. Most days I use the newsagent and the betting shop, and I go in the Albert quite often since that's right opposite. I drop into the bookshop occasionally, though I don't buy books because I don't have time to read them. There are several moves on now for other places to be open at night on the Lane, restaurants and more wine bars, and so on. I welcome the competition, but I think it would be a pity if the night life took over the Lane too much, because part of its charm is the variety of its shops. We don't want that to go.

Patrick outside Keith's. TW

22. Mrs. Ruth Heague. Manageress of The Masonic

The Masonic is the second pub in the Lane and the rival of the Albert. It is a Tetley's pub, serving real ale. The manageress, Mrs. Heague, enjoys the Lane but hopes one day to move to the country.

Mrs. Heague:

The majority of customers go between the two pubs. We have real ale and manual pumps, partly because this is the type of thing students go for and about 60 are students.

You have to remove people all the time. I do it myself. We get the local drunks here, you know, who can't get served anywhere, but they always try. It does get funny at times.

Trade is quite good at present. When I first came into the Lane it was terrible. We have pool tables now, so darts went out. You've got to be on the go all the time to keep it the way you want it.

Ruth Heague with Maureen Ware, Doreen Grant and Fred Heague.

I started off in printing, did an apprenticeship from 14-18 and worked until I had my first child when I was 21. I had two years at home out of work, then I went back. I think boredom's got a lot to do with it. I worked in British Home Stores for a while, then as a barmaid for a long time. My husband Fred was working as a fitter's mate, and I was out of a night, and it was about then that I decided it would be better to run a pub myself. I have a very good mum who helps look after the children.

Jean Udy *(left)*, with her daughter Carol. Jean was a beloved barmaid at the Masonic. TW

I read all the papers, the *Mirror, Post, Echo,* and *News of the World*. The only time I get to read anything longer is on holiday, when I might read a Catherine Cookson.

I don't want to stay here forever. We have two dogs and a horse, which we keep stabled over on the Wirral. I'd like to move to the countryside eventually.

Comment by Stephen Banks:

My local was the Mace, myself and my two brothers drank there. Our parents were regulars in the Albert. They drank there back in the day when you would press the bell on the wall for the barmaid to take your order. How times have changed!

The Mace was a fantastic pub and I have very fond memories of the many characters that drank there. I remember many of the landlords, but my favourites were Ruth and Freddie Heague, who are still very good friends of mine.

23. Danny Kay. Publican of The Albert Hotel

Danny has been working on the Lane for eight years. Eventually he would like to move further out into the country.

Danny Kay:

The Albert opened about 107 years ago, the year after the Park gates. The rooms were all oak paneled and the bar had three different sections. And there were stables at the back, they're now a bottle store. We have three bars now plus a snooker room. We get quite a mixture of people, but we try to keep it quiet, no juke boxes for instance. I had one put in three or four years back, but then a petition went out so I got rid of it. We have a friendly rivalry with

Albert Hotel

the Masonic down the Lane. One night down there they asked how many people there had been refused service at the Albert, and I believe there were forty-two hands.

I came here eight years ago from Wigan. That pub had only one servery. The first night in there a fellow went out with 27 stitches on his forehead. Like a Wild West show, that was. This is a pretty quiet pub; you might get trouble one night a month. It used to be a Cain's pub, now it belongs to Tetley Walker. I reckon we get about 75 regulars and quite a good passing trade.

I started off as a farm labourer in Cheshire and left there when I was about nineteen. Then I went on the building trade as a labourer. Then we got wintered off, a bit of bad weather, so we moved up to St. Helens and I got a job at Pilkington's. I was there just over eight years. Did glass cutting and everything there, working as a subsidiary of a trained journeyman. Then Pilkington's had a strike and there were a few of us finding it difficult to get a job. I took over the Black Horse in Wigan after four or five different jobs in twelve months. They'd had six managers there in a fortnight. The first night there, as I said, we had trouble. There were these seven Irish brothers, and they started laying into somebody at twenty to eleven. Well, I called the police in, but I didn't say who'd caused the trouble. The next night when they turned up, I told them they were banned, but because they knew I hadn't turned them into the police they never gave any more trouble.

I've always been interested in meeting people, and eventually I'd like to get back and run a country pub. It's varied work, and part of your job is a pleasure. The wife runs the women's darts team, and I

Danny Kay, publican at the Albert. TW

play golf, pool, and darts. I like doing crosswords, mostly in the Daily Express and the Sunday Mirror. I did a lot of reading while working at Pilkington's, not so much now, but I like Kyle Onstott. I like to have a bet each day down at John Barbour's, and I always read the racing pages in the Express.

I have a sister of seventeen who can't get a job. The shortage of money all round is pretty clear. When you get a price increase, people still buy the same amount. They come in a bit later and spend that, a fiver or two or whatever, and then bugger off again. They haven't got much option.

Rita, a barmaid at the Albert. TW

24. Derek Murray. Antique Shop

(and 1979 cofounder of Larks in the Park, free concerts in Sefton Park)

Denyze and Mandy, performers at Larks in the Park. TW

Musician (sax and vocals) Denyze Alleyne-Johnson (on left) says:

On stage in Larks in the Parks around 1980 or 1981 with my band Zaleout. I'd been signed to Sire Records with a band called Dedbyrds/ Walkie Talkies. This was a new venture with a singer called

Mandarin Orange (right), who ended up playing violin with River Dance. We often frequented Keith's Bar, which was bustling with musicians and artists and lots of fun.

Derek Murray:

This was a chandler's before I took it over, they sold pet food and paraffin and all that sort of thing. I don't have a lease, if you like I'm subletting from the previous tenant for the first six months. The owner had a second shop down on Mill St, and I don't think there's room on the Lane for two chandlers. Their main competition was Harrison's. If you look above the door you can see there are three chickens there, which suggests that at one time this was perhaps a butcher's, or a poulterer's.

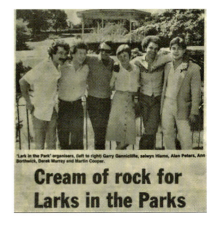

Derek Murray and fellow creators of Larks in the Park.

I've lived in the Lark Lane area for the past eight years. I lived in Pelham Grove first, then in East Albert Road, and I'm now in Linnet Lane. I was born in London, brought up in Derbyshire, and for me Lark Lane is Liverpool.

Before I came here, I was self-employed and working freelance mainly. I suppose the bulk of my time was spent making radio programmes for Radio City. I was doing a community magazine program called 'Connection', and I also did contributions for the weekend arts program. I've been Liverpool-based for about eight years and done a lot of community work. I worked at the Caribbean Centre and before that at the Victoria Settlement.

It was pure chance that brought me into the antique business. I went to a friend of mine and saying 'What can I do for one or two days a week that will leave me time to do my own thing and give me enough money to pay the bills?'. I went in with him, and we started buying a few things, stripping pine furniture, then I started buying bits of architecture, columns and fireplaces and doors from demolition firms and selling them within the trade. And then this shop fell vacant, so that seemed the next step.

The shop pays for itself now, covers my transport and provides a base for me to work from. It puts you on the map, and it provides a very basic living of about £30 a week. Where I make money is by acquiring a specific piece for a specific client or dealer. For instance, the glass in the window was acquired in Scotland and has been put on display, but in fact it's not for sale because I'm going to take it over to a dealer in Manchester who will take it and pay up without any problems. If I just left it in the shop it might take me much longer to sell it.

I wouldn't actually call myself an antique dealer. I think we deal more in taste, catering for particular kinds of taste. I only buy what I like, and I always work out in advance how much I have to make on a particular piece and who I can sell it to.

Lark Lane is the hub of my Liverpool, and it's this that keeps me here. For the kind of lifestyle I like, the physical environment here, squeezed between two parks, is important. And very close to the river, that's important to me too, just being able to hear the foghorn. Then the proliferation of trees, all the greenery, that makes it possible to live here without feeling that you're living in a big dirty, horrible, old, provincial city.

That's not to say that you go around with your eyes closed oblivious to social problems and stresses and pressures that to some extent everyone within Liverpool, and every major city, may be living under. But it's an environment which can be enjoyed, and an environment which the people within the area are now beginning to care more about, and not just preserve and restore.

I suppose it's a little Bohemian or trendy, and when people say the area's really coming on, they're referring to that aspect of it. But the real beauty of the area is the very mixed nature of the community. Some of the businesses of the Lane have been here for thirty or forty years. And then there's people like myself who've been here for a few months. And yet we all relate to each other; we can all get on. The Traders' Association is very active and organises things for our mutual benefit for the area as a whole.

The Lark Lane I know only came into existence five or six years ago with the blocking-off of the end of the Lane. I think that made the area into a little village. I think it has a great future, but there is a danger of it becoming overbalanced. The architecture of the area dictates a certain balance, and now most of the big houses have been converted into flats, which for the most part house an under-30 population. This has brought a great influx of younger people into the area. But it's a good thing for the area, because five to ten years ago a lot of this property was just lying derelict.

I can virtually live on the Lane; it's got most of what I need. I probably have breakfast at the Sunshine Café three or four mornings a week. I get papers delivered from Barnetts, the Times, and the New Statesman. I use the upholsterers, Callisters, for business, I use the florist for flowers for the shop. I don't get my hair cut on the Lane, because I have yet to find a white barber that can cut black hair successfully! I had it cut once on the Lane, and it was probably the worst haircut I ever had. Obviously, Keith's Wine Bar is a favourite haunt. I must go in there at least three times a week, and have done ever since they opened. I use both pubs at least twice a week. The antique shops, we all buy and sell between each other. I use the bookshop infrequently because I don't read a lot.

I live in a housing cooperative flat belonging to the Lark Lane Housing Co-op. Take the housing cooperatives, it's the way people do things in this area which counts. And we try to do our bit. For instance, we had a woman who came in and wanted a mirror to go with an old sideboard. We had one which was about the right size and shape but was the wrong colour. So, we arranged to strip it down for her, then we took it round to the house with a French polisher and he matched the colour up. I think this is typical of business around here, you can still get others to relate to you as people, not just straight forward take your money and run.

25. Kevin Hessey. Shoe Repairer

Kevin Hessey followed his father into this trade, and is the only shoe repairer on the Lane.

Kevin Hessey:

I knew Lark Lane as a kid and always liked it. I've been working there for nine months. One reason that made me decide to come here was that there were no other shoe repairers on the Lane.

I used to sag school a lot from Sefton Park School and I used to go to the Park every day with a few of my mates. We always came down Lark Lane for our chips. I was caught on several occasions round by the cricket ground and taken back to school, but dinner hour and I'd be away again. My dad got pinched, he got fined £25, I think.

There was a big family bust-up when we were kids, and we three lads stayed with my dad. He worked as a shoe-repairer too, and my eldest brother is in the same trade now. My dad opened his first shop off the Smithdown Road when he was 21. He met my mum in a coffee bar in Lark Lane. Now it's the Sunshine Café, but then it was a place where the bikers used to hang out.

When I left school, I went straight into this trade, you see I'd grown up with it. We were in Windsor Street, then Lawrence Road, and my dad's got a big shop off Park Road, with about twenty men.

I worked out at Ford's in Halewood for seven years, but I prefer working for myself, you have far more responsibility. And I can earn more here on a Saturday than in a whole week at Fords. I don't have a lot of expenses because I'm divorced. I get myself a nice pork chop at night, and then I have my bike. I have a car too, but I can't get it to go. I'm 27 and I belong to a bike club.

I have strong views on unemployment, you know half of them don't want to work. They're quite happy on the dole, there's some round here drawing £60 a week. I never had the slightest difficulty getting a job because I'd take anything, but these fellows won't do that. And you never hear that on television.

I've had three major accidents on my motor cycle so I laid off them for about four years. But when I got divorced, I thought I'd get one again. I read the *Motor Cycle News*, and apart from that I like war books mostly.

Kevin Hessey, *left*, and friend. TW

26. L'Alouette. French Restaurant

A French restaurant outside the city center is a rarity in Liverpool, and this one quickly established a regular following, even though its prices are not cheap. It was set up a year ago by an adventurous foursome – Vivienne and Arthur Wilson, and Michael and Beatrice Morley.

Group comments:

We'd been living locally and knew the area. We'd been looking for a place, and when this came up, we were attracted by its appearance. It had been a quality antique shop run by Mr. Jimmy Martin and his sister Miss Hilda. When he died, she carried on singlehanded until it got too much for her.

The Four at l'Alouette. *From left*: Arthur, Beatrice, Vivienne, and Michael.

The large plate glass windows were put in about forty years ago, according to Miss Hilda, when it was the Sefton Park Furnishing Store. On our opening night the windows got all steamed up, so we tried to dry them off with electric fans. But one got jammed right up against a window, and it split right down the middle. When we were thinking of setting up a restaurant, we realised that this huge dormitory of South Liverpool has almost nowhere to go if you're interested in good food except into town, where there are parking problems. We thought this would be easier, and we like the fact that this area is cosmopolitan.

It's a very friendly area, with a lot of old people living on this side of the Lane who've been here all their lives. And on the other side, where all the flats are, there is a moving population of students and other people. But everyone seems to get on well with each other. Our customers come from everywhere. We have quite a lot of regulars, and don't need to rely on advertising. Saturday is our consistently busiest night, but it can get very busy during the week.

Vivienne:

I was born in Liverpool, got married when I was 21, and have worked in about twenty different jobs. I had two children, then came back to work about four years ago as a part-time waitress and barmaid. I gained useful experience by working at a French restaurant in town, and now I work here for about three days and a couple nights a week.

Arthur:

I was born in Liverpool. I held various labouring jobs, went away to the Merchant Navy for three years, came back to Liverpool and worked here, and down in Hastings as a builder. I've also worked on the Channel ferries, and I ran a taxi cab here in Liverpool. Now I do the cooking, which I love. We also have to do the buying from the vegetable market, the fish market, and the meat market. It can be a bit of a bore, trailing around to get something if it's in short supply.

In my spare time I read anything I can get my hands on, mainly modern American fiction such as Kurt Vonnegut. I never use the library but I like to buy my own books and use the Lark Lane Bookshop a lot. That's partly out of loyalty, since the people there are neighbours of ours in Grove Park, but I also buy stuff for my two children there. They're aged seven and ten, and I read to them every night.

Michael:

I was born in Manchester, and moved to Liverpool with my family. Until last year I was teaching French in a comprehensive school. It's a very pleasant change from the classroom to a restaurant. I had become bored with teaching, and this is a completely different lifestyle. I still speak French occasionally; I suppose we get about one French customer a week. We had the French Consul in here once, but he didn't come back. Perhaps he didn't like the food.

Beatrice:

I grew up in France, and went to about five different lycées. They were run by very strict nuns, and I was always being expelled for answering back. Then I took a degree in philosophy and English at the University of Rouen. After that I came as a Lectrice to Liverpool University, and met Mike. I decided to come back to Liverpool, and for several years I worked as an Assistant in various local schools. I had once wanted to run a restaurant in France, and about five years ago Mike and I first began to think about opening one here. I worked for a year in a French restaurant here to gain some experience. It was my idea to call our place L'Alouette, which is the French for lark, it just seemed an obvious choice.

FOOD ON THE LANE

Menu L' Alouette

Hors d'ouevres

Soup du jour	
Pate with toast and gherkins	£0.90
Assiette de crudités	£1.15
Assiette de charcuterie	£1.10
Salade niçoise	£1.15
Salade au Roquefort	£1.05
Oeuf mayonnaise	£0.70
Avocat	£0 75
Saumon fumé	£1.60
Escargots de Bourgogne	£2.30
Coquilles St. Jacques	£2.50

Poissons et fruits de mer

Brochettes de coquilles St. Jacques au beurre blanc	£4.65
Thon au sauce castell	£4.75
Raie a la crème et aux capres	£4.50
Lotte	
Sole au pernod	£5.50

Viandes et volailles

Filet beurre maître d'hôtel	£5.50
Filet au poivre flambé au cognac	£5.50
Brochettes maison	£4.90
Poulet a l'estragon	
Poulet cocotte grand 'mere	£4.30
Escalope de veau vallee d'Auge	£5.10
Escalope du veau normande	£5.35
Veau normande flambé	
Plat de fromages	£0 80
Desserts	
Café	
Liqueur coffee	£1.20

27. Dr. Julian Kenyon. Non-invasive medicine

Dr. Kenyon first became familiar with the area as a student, and he now lives and works here. He played a major part in the early discussions that led to the setting up of the community association, and he is also interested in conservation.

Dr. Kenyon:

We moved into the area in 1974, after getting to know it as a student. Our house is in Alexandra Drive, and I use this magnificent house on Aigburth Drive as a base for my work. I used to be a surgeon, but I resigned fifteen years ago from lecturing in the university, since I found that very limiting. Now I work in non-invasive medicine, which includes acupuncture.

I trained in acupuncture in China. I read one or two important authors who changed my thinking, especially Ivan Ilich, and I withdrew from allopathic medicine. I now have people coming to see me from all over the country, and this is a convenient base, not far from the airport.

I have a very strong feel for Lark Lane. This area is probably one of the very few which is still much as it was a hundred years ago. And once people move in here, they tend to feel strongly committed. My own interest was initially mainly in conservation, but now I'm also involved in the social aspects. There is still a lot of dereliction, and a threat that the area could become a geriatric desert. We need to have more young families moving in, but until recently it has been difficult to finance property around here.

I try and support the Lane as much as possible. You do pay a little bit more, but the Lane is the heart of the area. There had been a division of opinion within the Community Association; one group is against the holding of antique fairs there, since they feel that the centre should not be involved with commercial ventures. But when the Urban Aid grant stops in a few years the area must become commercially viable.

One of the good things about the Community Association is that it enables you to associate with lots of different kinds of people. It's emphatically not a middle-class ghetto. In some ways the make-up of the area is still close to what it was fifty years ago, though of course there have been some changes for the good.

I tend to see development round here in global terms. What we are seeing everywhere is the collapse of the big organisations and the shifts over to thinking small. The rightness of banding together is more important, I believe, than the success of the enterprise.

Dr. Julian Kenyon.

28. Jane and James Baxter. Mechanical engineer, antique car expert and community organiser

Jane and James (Jim) Baxter have a keen interest in the history of the area, and Jane is honorary secretary of the Lark Lane Traders' Association. James has been living in Lucerne Street for twenty years, and runs an antique car business. Their house is the first shippon built by Hogg's Dairy, and churn marks can still be seen on the side of the stairs. James describes himself as a kind of village blacksmith performing a whole variety of tasks, from letting people into houses they've locked themselves out of, to mending broken toys for children. Before and after WW2, Mr. Baxter was in charge of Pollard's garage in Ullet Rd., 'the most expensive workshop in town'. He remembers with what deference the gentry were once treated:

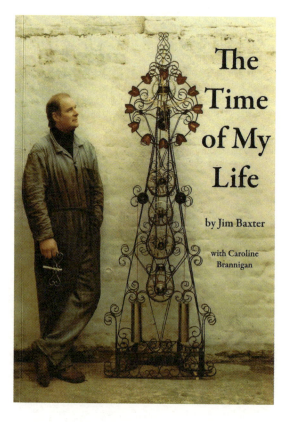

Memoir by Jim Baxter.

A View of the Motor Museum, mid-1980s.

Jim Baxter:

The people who lived round the Park were very special kinds of people. I used to mend punctures on their cars, and then wash the wheels before the cars were taken back.

Mrs. Jane Baxter describes the gradual revival of a community spirit on the Lane:

We lived for a few years with the threat of the bulldozer. It came pretty close, the next street in fact. When we knew we were safe, we were so relieved that a lot of people began to take a new pride in their properties. We were able to get grants, and realised how fortunate we were.

The City Planner came down here one day and started looking thoughtful. My husband told him that he'd better not start planning anything, that we were happy the way we are. And that was a bit of a turning point. At that time, not just here, but everywhere in

Jim and Jane Baxter with their Lancia Lambda at the Palm House.

Liverpool was coming under the bulldozer, whether it was habitable or not. Wholesale demolition was going on, and plots were lying empty for years and years.

A lot of interest in the community began when we celebrated the Queen's Jubilee. That brought out a terrific feeling, and we haven't looked back since then. Our New Year parties in the street and such things have had something about them since that event. It's a pity we don't have more of that sort of thing to get people together.

The Lark Lane Traders' Association was begun four or five years ago by Mr. Daniels. It took quite a bit of work to get it off the ground, but it's a very useful organisation.

When the underpass was built, it cut off passing trade, but now the Lane seems to be on the 'up' again. At the moment it has a bit of an aura about it, it's an 'in' place for arty, or slightly off-beat types. But there's also lots of environmental work going on down at the community centre. We're gradually pulling ourselves up by our bootlaces. Most of the derelict properties are now being done up, converted into flats and so on by housing cooperatives.

Comment by Andrew Butterfield:

We played football for SMLLCA located in the Old Police Station. We were sponsored by Jim and Jane Baxter, who paid for our new kits. Lark Lane Motor Museum was opened by the Baxters in the former Charlett's funeral directors' premises. It was open to the public, and had every conceivable motor memorabilia you could get. To name a few vintage cars: an Austin A7 used as a wedding car, a Model T Ford, fuel pumps, vintage toys. An absolutely fab place! Unfortunately, after a very successful launch, the number of visitors dried up and it closed. Such a pity!

Update by KF, 2020:

In 2018 Jim Baxter published a wonderful memoir, *The Time of My Life*, with memoir writer Caroline Brannigan. It is filled with madcap and witty anecdotes by Jim and Jane, demonstrating how Jim has applied his brilliant mechanical and design skills in many different directions, from clocks to motorcycles, to Paralympic wheelchairs.

The chapter 'Larks at the Museum', tells the story of the Motor Museum. It also shows the couple's key role in driving a student-initiated campaign from 1992 to restore the by then 'elderly, decaying, majestic' Palm House in Sefton Park. A £10.00 Sponsor a Pane scheme raised £45,000 to replace the 3712 panes of glass, and led to successful major funding from the National Lottery. Jane wrote the newsletter to members from May 1995 to October 2000, and the restored building was reopened in 2001. Their patron was the jazz musician and local resident George Melly, a great-nephew of the original Park visionary Charles Pierre Melly. On the Opening Day, Jim sat next to Melly on the marble bench along with another volunteer, sharing a bottle of whisky. Now the Palm House Trust carries the work forward.

'Life has been a great adventure' laughs Jim. Thank you for your great civic spirit, Jim and Jane.

29. Helen Prescott. Editor of *Creative Mind*

Helen Prescott is concerned with fostering an interest in the arts in the community. She sees her function as that of a coordinator, enabling others to get things going. She firmly believes that the Liverpool 'revival' is on, and thinks of the town as one of the first 'post-industrial' cities.

Creative Mind founder and editor Helen Prescott. c.2004/05.

Helen Prescott:

My own particular interest is in running an arts association called Creative Mind, which is just moving into new offices in the Community Centre. We publish a quarterly magazine under the same name which has details of arts, ecology, alternative technology and mysticism. It's an alternative publication and began in December 1978. I do most of the work, and we are mainly financed by advertising. I don't pay myself a salary, and technically I'm unemployed. I'm hoping we can interest a foundation like the Gulbenkian in our activities.

I've been in Liverpool for seven or eight years. I first came to the university and then, like many people, I stayed. I studied philosophy and then psychology. Before the Community Centre was set up, we already had a base in town, in Mathew Street, and then in a warehouse in Manesty's Lane. But I like the sense of community here in what I call Lark Lane Village.

We are particularly concerned about getting community arts going for the 22-35 age group. There are lots of artistic people living around here, but so far, the community has placed a far stronger emphasis on children's playgroups and activities for the old people. We are aiming at the age group in the middle. We've set up our own film society, arranged concerts, and got classes going in photography and pottery. And we're hoping that the new office will help us to set up a kind of centre for consciousness, with popular lectures and seminars.

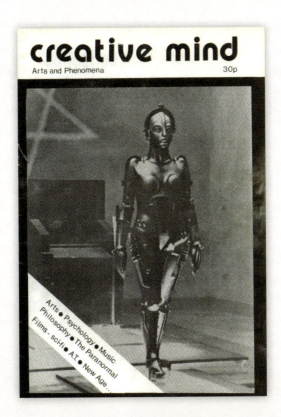

Creative Mind, #1, 1979.

Helen Prescott. Update from December 2019
Remembering the Lane in the 1970s and '80s.

When I arrived in the Lane in 1975, it was a quiet village-type place and very unspoilt. I lived just off Lark Lane on Linnet Lane which runs parallel to Sefton Park. First, I dwelt at Number 26, then moved to the very attractive house at Number 3, where I occupied the entire first floor until 1988. David Backhouse, the architect who designed Cavern Walks, also lived at Number 3, in the coach house round the back. People often remember me from those days due to the dog I had that looked like a fox as she streaked across the Park. My dog Sheppie and I lived there for many years.

I'd studied philosophy and psychology at Liverpool University, then went on to study Jungian Psychology at the Jung Institute in Zurich with Marie Louise von Frank and James Hillman, the two leading Jungians of the age. In my other role I was both a Wittgenstein scholar and Philosopher of Mind.

As I ran *Creative Mind* from Lark Lane, hundreds of people would drop round to see me, with many of them staying over. I even made some life-long friends from my Lark Lane office including a couple visiting from the Isle of Man. David Stevens often visited, and Bob Wooler would drop by to read me the songs he had written. He wanted me to put them to music.

I arranged for Satish Kumar, the editor of *Resurgence*, to come to Liverpool on his Peace March. He visited Lark Lane and stayed with me, as did many others. The list is too long to mention but they include Francis Huxley, (nephew of Aldous), Stan Gooch, former child psychologist and author of many books including *Total Man*. Peter Russell, the amazing English-Italian poet came. He'd been Professor of English at Tehran University when the rebels invaded the city. He was in a house attacked by gunmen and hid in the attic. They massacred the entire household bar him!

John Papworth, editor of *Fourth World* also came. I wrote pieces for both *Resurgence* and *Fourth World* plus many other publications, including editing and writing for my own *Creative Mind*, which remained in publication until 2008.

Most of those who came to visit me at Lark Lane were intrigued as to what Creative Mind was, or they arrived due to our shared interests in philosophy and psychology.

Apart from producing the Arts magazine, I also ran arts events and workshops like poetry readings. Also, art/psychology events like Mandala workshops or Dreams workshops. *Creative Mind* conferences had a philosophical base and put on a handful of 3-D movies like 'Creature from the Black Lagoon'. I also had a slot on local radio interpreting people's dreams or discussing issues like 'sinistry' which is lefthandedness. This tied in with my work with Stan Gooch.

My Friendship with Dr. Julian Kenyon

I was great friends with Julian. We had the same sense of humour and were both Pisces! I always found Julian very easy going, engaging and an honest individual. At one stage we contemplated building a Wilhelm Reich 'Orgone Accumulator Box' in his back garden so we could all get psychically charged up! Wonderful stuff! I was equally a friend of Margaret, Julian's wife, as she also had an interest in New Age activities and alternative medicine. I was also friends with his brother Chris Kenyon, who lived off Lark Lane and also went into medicine.

Like Julian, I'd read Illich and others and had a keen interest in alternative treatments. At the time I was in communication with both R.D. Laing and Francis Huxley. I got Laing to write a piece for *Creative Mind*. When Francis visited Liverpool, he thought I 'might have something.' I believe Julian was still a member of Lark Lane during the '80s but he was very busy with his acupuncture practice then. He had a magnificent magnolia tree in his garden.

30. David Gibbon. Building Surveyor

This family got to know the district while students, and have since bought an old house in Hadassah Grove. They are active in the Community Assn.

David Gibbon:

We bought this house in 1977. A Mrs. O'Leary had died here a few years before and the house was completely derelict. She had lived here with her mother from around the Second World War. The house changed hands a number of times in the 19th century, and then hardly at all this century.

I think this house was originally owned by the chap who built the Grove. The deeds described someone who was a clerk in holy orders as living in this house later on. I don't know why it was called Hadassah Grove. But there were Welsh builders working here, and the Welsh are biblically oriented. I know that Hadassah is another form of Esther.

As a student, and after graduating, I lived in various houses in Liverpool 8. Then one Sunday afternoon we came for a walk down here and saw this derelict house. We sort of peered in, the garden was a complete wilderness, about six feet high with brambles.

I'm a building surveyor, so doing up old houses is my line, and this seemed an attractive proposition to take on. Then we badgered the owners for about a year until they finally sold it to us.

I got involved in the Lark Lane Community Association in around 1978. They were already in the Old Police Station, and the job creation scheme was just getting under way, trying to put the place in order. It was unused as a community centre at that stage. We were still talking about all the things we might do to get it off the ground. I've been most involved in the building side of it, the fabric, but I'm interested in the whole thing. I'm keen to get it developing all sides of community life. At one time we felt as if we were only doing things for young kids, so I and others pointed to the need to do more for the old age pensioners, for the people in the middle, and for the older kids.

When the group started off, I think everybody thought of themselves as being members of what you would roughly define as the alternative culture. I think I've become progressively turned against it. I would far rather see the long-term indigenous people of the neighbourhood be the backbone of the community association, and to see us doing things for the working-class community of St. Michael's than exclusively as a club for the alternative people.

That's one of the attractions of it to me. There are many areas of Liverpool where people are fiercely competitive about their class position the whole time. You come across people who live in Formby and on the Wirral who have not a notion of what working-class people are like. They keep themselves completely isolated. But here, people are more mixed up together. Obviously, that produces a certain amount of tension, but that's not a bad thing.

It's difficult to know if there will be any significant gentrification of the area in the future. Middle-class people with pure middle-class interests wouldn't come and live here. You have to be slightly peculiar. When you boil it down, there just isn't enough of the right kind of accommodation available, especially houses with good-sized gardens. If you look at the houses in many of the roads around here, you will find they are so large that they dwarf the garden. Somehow in the nineteenth century houses just weren't built with enough land round them.

I do wish we could somehow organise it to bring in more family accommodation. I think that the idea of a conservation area is a bit restricting really. If there was pressure for development, and a desire to pull down some of the bigger Victorian houses of no great distinction and to replace them with low-cost family housing instead, I'm fairly sure that would strengthen the area tremendously. All this bedsitter-land stuff is a bit uniform; I think you need families to create a community.

People should remember that many shopping streets like Lark Lane have gone into extinction in Liverpool and elsewhere, and for it to find some way of surviving is all to the good. If Lark Lane becomes a specialist street with antique shops and restaurants and wine bars then fine, competition helps little shops to stay alive. The alternative is dereliction.

I still attend Christ Church in Linnet Lane, though it's a bit depressing in some ways attending a church built for 800. Five or six years ago its congregation was down to about a dozen. Now, it's up to a regular Sunday attendance of around 60-70. But I think a new swing back to the churches is bound to happen in the next few years, you can already see signs of an upswing on a national level.

Garden at 19 Hadassah Grove, early 1980s.

31. Mr. Alan Hoyte. Hesketh Street Housing Cooperative

Many of the old houses in the area are currently being renovated and made suitable for multiple occupancy by various housing associations. These include the Lark Lane Housing Co-op and the Hesketh Street Housing Co-op, which is taking a major share in the new housing development on the site of the old terrace housing in Hesketh Street. Mr. Hoyte has taken part in the discussions from the beginning, and also works full-time for local housing associations.

Alan Hoyte:

I went to university at Sheffield, then worked for about twelve years in advertising and marketing. Gradually, I began to realise that there was something more to life than just working in a mundane job, and politically I was out of sympathy because I was working for a monopoly at the time. I thought about lecturing, and did a one-year Management Studies postgraduate course at the Liverpool Poly, but I soon found that jobs were very hard to come by since when people left, they just weren't being replaced.

By that time, I'd begun to get involved in the Hesketh Street scheme. Our prime objective in forming the co-op was to save a group of houses in the street which were due for demolition. After forming the co-op in 1977 we tried to keep the houses afloat, but that failed and it was then decided that we would try and secure the land and build new houses on it. We then ran into political difficulties, partly because of a lack of liaison with our agents, the Neighbourhood Housing Services.

Finally, after a lot of hassle it was agreed that the Co-operative Services Development Organisation of Bold Street would have 20 units in order to rehouse people from their clearance area over in High Park area in Liverpool 8, and that we would have 10 units.

I've also been a member of Lark Lane Co-op for several years. It's a very slow process, and until December 1980 we didn't have anything to show for it. Then No. 15 Linnet Lane was completed and our first tenants moved in. There are now quite a few other properties in the pipeline in West Albert and South Albert Road.

We had discussions about future tenants from the outset. Many of the old people who were living in Hesketh Street have now been rehoused near Otterspool, and they don't fancy moving twice. So, we've had to reallocate properties. We set up a committee, but we also call general meetings to decide on architects and other issues.

At present I live in a flat. I was forced into selling my home when I took the course at the Poly. From a personal point of view the Hesketh Street Housing Co-op was the best thing that ever happened to me. Since I'm a member, that qualifies me for a house, and we'll be moving into a four-bed house there, living with all our friends and with 40' of garden.

My wife has spent all her life in this area and went to St. Michael's. I had a two-up, two-down upbringing in Bootle, and my parents really struggled to get themselves a council house on a really magnificent five-star estate in Litherland. I think they deserved it. I love living around here, but my wife thinks it would be nice some day to move out of the town to some place like Newquay.

I think the Lane has taken off. Until a few years ago the phone exchange was its only claim to fame. Now perhaps there are too many trendies, but I don't mind. My view is live and let live.

32. Christ Church and Founding of Lark Lane Community Association (Christ Church)

On the Lane, Christ Church erected a Church Schools building and an Institute, both of which institutions were directed towards the working-class members of the parish. In 1921 a jubilee booklet estimated that a quarter of the population came from that sector, while the majority were middle class. In the 1960s both buildings on the Lane were sold because of shrinking population. However, the present Vicar, the Rev. A. Thomas, has played an active part in the reshaping of the community through helping to sponsor the idea of a new community centre.

Rev. Thomas:

When the church first began it was largely to serve the houses round the Park, and the servants came in the evening. Now, of course, the big houses are flats or bed-sitters, and the population is pretty mobile. Young people tend to come here to get themselves going while they're saving money to buy a house. Then when they've got the deposit together, off they go.

When I first came here in 1972 the parish was predominantly elderly. We now have quite a good group in the 20-40 age group, which is good. The old people are having to take notice of the younger people, and vice versa. But I've always regarded my situation here as a holding situation, until the area settles down. Ultimately, I think the area will probably be dominated by housing association work.

Bringing the Community Together

Back in 1975 Julian Kenyon and I called a meeting in the church hall to discuss setting up a community organisation, and so many people turned up – around 300 – that we had to switch it to the church. The strange thing was that that same night, unbeknown to either of us, a similar meeting was taking place in the Albert. That was a much smaller group, and they called themselves the

St. Michael's Ward Association. We tended to think in terms of this immediate area, and called ourselves the Lark Lane Association. Eventually the two groups got together, and we became the St. Michael's and Lark Lane Community Association. I became the vice chairman.

Then the Police Station came vacant, and we decided to go for that. I felt that it was a mistake to be taking over an old property like that, so I resigned, though I have continued to support the project. And it has turned out very well.

My Life Story

I was in the Gas Board before I entered the ministry. I did my training at St. Aidan's College in Birkenhead, and then started off at St. Andrew's in Kettering, which was probably the best attended church in the diocese then, in the late '50s. Then I came up here to do an Anglican-Methodist experiment on a new estate in Childwall. Unfortunately, nothing came of that. Then I moved for several years to St. Helen's, and then to here.

A while ago I was asked to give a talk at the Conservative Club on the problems of today's young people. I pointed out that one of the problems is that these young people have been brought up by a godless older generation. In a way, the sins of the parents are being visited upon the children.

Christ Church, Linnet Lane.

SIX OLDER RESIDENTS

Mr. Sam Evans. Gas fitter, with Mrs. Mary Evans

Mr. Sam Evans was born on the Lane in 1902 and worked as a gas fitter. Mrs. Evans was born in Disley, near Stockport, and moved to Lark Lane with her father, who was a plumber. She sat next to her future husband Sam at school at St. Michael's. Later Mrs. Evans worked at the dyers and cleaners' shop in the Lane, and in 1980 she was helping out in the kitchen at the Joseph Gibbon's Day Centre every week. Interview recorded in 1980.

Mr. Sam Evans:

I was born at 17 Bickerton Street, it's demolished now. It was a small terrace with two bedrooms and an outside privy. My father was a labourer who worked for several of the big families. He did gardening and window-cleaning. Years ago, it was like a village here. Most of the people were coachmen and gardeners. All the terrace houses, that was how they got their living.

Seventy years ago, I used to take newspapers out for the newsagent at the top of the Lane, and we used to get to know all the gentry round the Park. Going down Aigburth Drive, No. 2 was Clarkes, the tobacco people. Then there was Mrs. Adam, in the house called Belem Towers. In the front of the house was a big tower and she used to sit there and look right across the Park all day. She was old, you know, just like Queen Victoria.

They never mixed with you, you know. The sons used to come in the Lane and buy sweets. It was all high class at one time, high-class sweets. We used to tease them; they all had new bikes and

Mr. Sam Evans. Gas fitter, with Mrs. Mary Evans. TW

all that caper. But sometimes they'd loan you the bike to go around the block like, oh aye.

The first thing anybody thought about when a lad left school was, what shop are you going to work at? Well, I had it at the back of my mind, I wasn't having any shop lad job. I wasn't taking that kind of orders out any more. I'd worked from when I was about eight, at the newsagent's, and at the barber's, and at the cake shop, taking out orders and things like that. And I thought well, when my turn comes, I'd look around for something different. And one of the gentry round the park, he gave my mother a letter for me to take down to the Gas Board. That was in Duke Street in them days.

So, we went down there with this letter. But if I'd had a decent education, I could have got a better job than what I got. I served my time to a gas fitter. That took seven years, from fourteen until twenty-one.

I came out of my time on the tools, you know laying pipes and so on. Then I went to be an examiner and they put me in uniform. It was a good job, them days it was a plum job. It was a staff job, you got superannuation, you know. I took a drop when I went off the tools and became an examiner, I got about £3 a week. And uniform once a year. That was in the 1920s. We got married in 1926, and we've been married 54 years this March coming.

I was at the gas company 57 years and I enjoyed every minute of it. I was there an hour before my time every morning, and finished up as a path surveyor. If I had the say I'd go back tomorrow. The harder the problems, you know, the more I enjoyed it. I used to do a lot of drawings, you know, things like that. Surveying was the best part of the job. I used to do the work for the Corporation, new schools. Oh, I used to like it.

All the gentry went from the area before the war. There was only one family living in the Drive, a chap named Molyneux-Cohan. I was on the church council of Christ Church with him. I served on that for about forty years.

34. Miss Iva Jones of Lucerne Street:

I've lived in this area all my life, in Hesketh Street and then in Lucerne Street. I was eight when WW1 started, and I remember my eldest brother was away in the army in France. My father was a Shropshire man. He came here as a groom and became a coachman after. My mother was Manx. She worked in service as a cook in a house at the top of Bertram Road. In my early days my father became a cab driver. There were stables at the top of Lark Lane, and we would take my father's dinner up. Tuesday was Philharmonic night, that was always cabbie business.

My mother never worked after she was married. There were nine children. We just had three bedrooms, but the front bedroom is exceptionally big, it goes right across the front of the house. And one or two of my sisters were in service by the time I was born. One sister went back to Oswestry in retirement — the others all stayed. One in Wavertree, one in Cressington. My brothers lived in Garston, Allerton and Huyton. One of my sisters lived lower down in Lucerne Street, and another sister lived in the Dingle.

I went to school at St. Michael's, left when I was fourteen, and stayed at home a good long time. By that time Mother was getting a bit older. Then in 1930-31 I went into service. There were three of us there. The cook and the nurse lived in, but I always went home every night. The wages were 10 shillings a week, from half seven until after dinner at night. You had half a day off in the week, and Sundays as well until after lunch.

Later I went to work for St. Nicholas, the girls' club at the Pier Head. Lots of business girls went there, we had one room with Littlewoods girls. We loved going to the Rivoli Picture theatre, at the corner of

Rivoli Picture Theatre.

Tramway Road. We went to other girls' clubs, and the Band of Hope, which met at the Church Hall.

During WW2, I worked for Peyton Calvert, on what they called CIA government inspection. It was pretty grim here during the war. There was a land mine in Siddeley Street, and another one went off in Linnet Lane. There was also a direct hit at Belem Towers.

When the war was over, I went to the Automatic (Plessey's). I left there to go to Thornton's with a friend. After that I went back to the Automatic and retired from there, but I had broken service so I didn't get a pension. My stretch was about 21 years in all, but I had only 16 years together.

In the old days Charlett's took people off. Funerals went by without much fuss. Now it takes £400 to bury you in a mean way. A friend of mine had £240 stolen. She was saving it for her funeral.

This is a good area for older people. The young ones have changed but the older ones haven't. As far as the servants go, I suppose it's a good thing they've got rid of the old way of doing things, but for the atmosphere of the district it's not such a good thing. I've got students living opposite me now, they're a very nice quiet bunch.

Carriages at Sefton Park.

35. Mrs. Dora Ince of Burdett Street:
(born c. 1910, living in 1980 in Holt House)

My parents were both Liverpool born and bred. I was born in Burdett Street in St. Michael's. My father was a team owner. His stables were in Upper Warwick Street. My mother was always at home because she had ten children, seven girls and three boys. I was the seventh. When we lived in Upper Warwick Street, we had five bedrooms, so there was plenty of room.

I went to St. Margaret's School in Princes Road. I was quite good at school, I remember I got a book as a prize, called *True Stories of Girl Heroines*. We used to go to the Mayfair on Saturday afternoons for tuppence. I remember seeing Jessie Matthews when I was 13 or 14.

After leaving school I worked as a clerk. One of my sisters was a governess for a vicar in Pitt Street, and others worked in shops. My three brothers all worked for Father. I got married when I was about 24. My husband was a clerk. We rented a house in Burdett Street for 9/- or 10/- a week. I kept on working for a short time, and then had two sons. They both went abroad to look for better jobs.

Fuchsia,
Pelham Grove

36. Dr. Grace Gillespie and Bryce Gillespie – Two Careers in India and New Zealand

Dr. Grace Gillespie and her brother Bryce Gillespie were of Scottish descent and grew up around Lark Lane. Grace was born in 1899 and Bryce in 1900. Grace attended the Belvedere School, and then went on to study medicine at the University of Liverpool. 'I never wanted to be anything but a doctor,' she said in an interview in 1981.

Her early path was not easy. 'I started my studies, then had a breakdown and was off for five years.' After returning to medical school and qualifying in Liverpool, in 1928 she took up a position at the Mission Hospital (Holdsworth Memorial Hospital) in the town of Mysore (now Mysuru) capital of a kingdom for nearly six centuries, from 1399-1956. The hospital was associated with the Wesleyan Mission. There she rose to become head of the Women's Department, highly respected and loved.

Author Girija Madhavan opens her article 'Reminiscing Childhood Memories of Old Mysore' with this delightful anecdote:

Girija Madhavan.

Girija Madhavan:

I was born in 1938 in a house now called "Sahyadri," the first of the four large Railway Bungalows that still stand facing KRS Road in Vani Vilas Mohalla, diagonally opposite Cheluvamba Park. In those days, it was known as the Loco Superintendent's Bungalow. A Scotswoman, Dr. Gillespie of the Mission [or Holdsworth Memorial] Hospital, attended on the birth, in the front left bedroom with the window with wooden shade [called a 'Monkey Top']. The house was allotted to my father, M. Venkatesh, who was an engineer of the old 'Mysore State Railways.' It was a colonial bungalow set in a large garden of trees, flowering bushes and creepers. The cork tree painted

by my mother, artist Mukta Venkatesh, still retains its grace. I too like to paint our natural world.

Image: Girija Madhavan, Egrets in a Mysuru Lake. Watercolour, 2014.

In retirement, Grace returned to Lark Lane, to a home in Parkfield Road that she shares with her brother. She is still engaged in charitable work with the Needlework Guild.

Dr. Grace Gillespie:

We collect garments and give them to organised charities that need clothing. Gradually during these years it's faded out because of the Welfare State. There was a time when we collected around 7,000 a year. Now it's 300 garments and around 15 charities. I reckon that the people we used to think of as the poor and needy are the rich today!

Bryce Gillespie:

Bryce Gillespie started his education at a school in Parkfield Road, followed by boarding school in Cambridge. He is shocked when he recalls the upstairs/downstairs world of his childhood and the low wages of servants:

Our cook came to us when she was 15 or 16. She lived in, and we paid her a pound a week. It was appalling, really, when you think of it.

Bryce's varied career began by joining the Royal Flying Corps, and learning to fly biplanes during World War 1. He later spent many years teaching in New Zealand. 'I came back every seven years,' he said. Their house was built in 1912. After returning to Liverpool, he taught at Liverpool Collegiate School until retiring in 1965.

An undated article [1990] in the Liverpool Daily Post mentions that Grace passed away in 1988. In the same article, their niece Mrs. Alison Smythe mentions that on his 90th birthday veteran pilot Bryce was taken for a trip in a police helicopter from Liverpool Airport. He was a member of Toxteth United Reform Church.

A friend, Ken Harrison, Harry Lawrenson (known as Mr. Kidd), and Bryce Gillespie.

GROWING UP IN THE BIG HOUSES: SIX STORIES

37. Miss Joan Carey.   Games Mistress

Miss Carey is a daughter of Mr. Edward Carey, who was registrar of Liverpool University from 1913-1937. After her mother's death and her father's remarriage she was forced to become independent. It was a hard struggle.

Miss Carey:

I was born in 1902. My grandfather was secretary of the United Alkali Company, which later became part of ICI. He lived in Gateacre. My mother was one of eight children and her father was a clergyman in the Church of Ireland in Dublin. They used to go to Criccieth for their summer holidays, and that's where she met my father.

After their marriage they lived in 20 Alexandra Drive, and that's where I was born. South Liverpool School was on the corner of Sandringham Drive, and Summerfield School was also in the road. Later on, we moved to The Elms, which was a nice road in those days. We lived opposite the stables. There were six children, and I was the second eldest.

I first attended a small school run by Miss Katie Yates. It was above Sidley's, the stationers, at the end of Lark Lane. We were at that school when it moved to Marmion Road, and I think we were supposed to have helped to call it Camelot. I collected India rubbers in boxes. I loved their different colours, and I liked the feel of them. There was a lovely sweet shop opposite, White's, and I can still remember the look of the little Miss White.

Main building at Holly Lodge.

There were two delightful women in Stevenson's on the Lane. Mother used to take us shopping there, all three of us, all dressed alike. She made most of our clothes, I can remember we had red coats and red bonnets with ribbons. I was always dressed in dark clothes, and the other two wore lighter ones, because I was always dirty. I thought I ought to have been a boy.

Only one of us was allowed into Stevenson's, because the Miss Stevensons gave a piece of fudge to the one who went in. And it was lovely! And so of course we had to wait for three weeks to get our turn for the piece of fudge.

Later we went to the South Liverpool School, where our teachers were Miss Beaumont and Miss Bevan. Mother died in 1916 having the last baby, Faith. By then we had moved to St. Michael's-in-the-Hamlet, to *Westerland*, a lovely house which is now the Vicarage. We had stables and a swing and a trapeze.

After Mother's death, Father married the boys' governess, and we were sent to Huyton to boarding school. From then on it was grim. We loved boarding school, but I could never go home in the holidays. I had to borrow money from my aunt to do my last term at Huyton.

I wanted to become a games mistress. You must go either to Dartford or Bedford, they said. Bedford accepted me, but I would have had to wait a year and I couldn't afford that. So instead I went to the Liverpool Training College. My first job was up in Edinburgh. I earned £90 a year, £30 at the end of each term. Twenty went to pay back my debt, so I then had only ten pounds to live on for the rest of the next term. And I had to get jobs in the holidays, because I couldn't go home.

Then I got a job at Holly Lodge Grammar School in West Derby, and I stayed there until I retired.

It was a lovely school in my day, with a wonderful headmistress. We had four hockey pitches and thirteen tennis courts. It was a lovely job, because I like the young. And the last five years I was at the school, they won the whole of the Lancashire Schools' hockey tournament! I retired at 60, but went on teaching part-time until I was 67, and thoroughly enjoyed it.

I was 25 before I ever went out with a man. And of course, missed the bus entirely! I was always hefty, I was 12 stone 4 lb. when I was 19. So, I never really thought anyone could fall for someone as hefty. So, there you are, you see. I'd have liked to be married because I liked kids. But you can't have everything in life, and now I'm on the better wicket. So many of my friends are widows, and they're really desolate, whereas I've had to make my own life.

Comments by Holly Lodge old girls:
On the school:

Lorna Moffatt: Holly Lodge took girls from all over Liverpool who had passed the 11+. Quite a large school, more than 500 pupils. The Head was Miss Ingram, always known as Dolly. She was strict but fair and knew all by name. As Head girl in 1964-65 I had to see her first thing every morning for my instructions, so I got to know her quite well and became quite fond of her. She lived in a flat upstairs in Uplands, one of the Holly Lodge buildings.

On Miss Carey:

Jane Dow: I was at HL 1962-67. Miss Carey was my P.E. teacher, never knew her name was Joan! Miss Carey was a typical old-type school teacher, strict and no nonsense. I played in both hockey and netball teams, but my overriding memory is that we had to do gym in navy blue knickers. Miss Carey would supply them if you forgot yours, but they had HLHS embroidered across the bum in big red letters!!!

Irene Vickers: I was there 1960 to 1968. I remember Miss Carey well. Yes, she could be quite firm and strict, always wanted us to win, whatever the cost. I think she was well thought of by the Head as the school excelled in every sport. It also had amazing facilities. For a city girl, it was like going to school in the countryside. I remember the duck pond, a beautiful vista in all the seasons. Also the tennis courts, which were down the path past Uplands, surrounded by trees. Sandheys in the snow overlooking the back lawns. So many beautiful picturesque areas! Strict school, but I enjoyed my time there immensely.

Susan Milce Quinlan, née Milce: I remember Miss Carey as being strict but fair, and highly respected. I was a pupil from 1961-66 and played hockey. My twin brother and I passed the scholarship at the same time, so having to buy two uniforms etc., was a real financial burden for my parents.

One day Miss Carey took me to one side and said she knew my family was short of money, so I could pay for my hockey stick weekly. It's always puzzled me how she knew that, as I had the same uniform as everyone else and didn't qualify for free school meals.

When she retired, Miss Carey had a standing ovation at the Philharmonic that went on for a long time.

Many years later – about 1985 – I ran into her on the street and stopped to talk to her. She thanked me for stopping and talking, which I found quite touching.

Shirley Ann Cheyne: I attended Holly Lodge, 1961-68 and Miss Carey was the head games mistress, strong but very kind. Years later, early to mid 90s I was RGN at a residential and nursing home near Sefton Park when Miss Carey took up residence with us. She was a delight to spend time with and was still very kind with a brilliant sense of humour. Her passing left a great gap for the staff and myself. I've never met anyone else with her strength, bravery and lust for life. We all missed her but life was richer for having known her, bless her memory.

38. Miss K. Rutherford

Miss Rutherford's fondest memory of growing up around the Lane is of playing tennis at the Mersey Bowmen Tennis Club in Sefton Park. After attending boarding school in Wales Miss Rutherford returned to Liverpool and stayed at home, doing charity work and following the accepted role for middle-class girls in that period. Looking back, she laughs when she remembers she found a cookery class a waste of effort because she believed there would always be servants to look after her. The social changes in the country and the district disturb her. Her older sister Gladys, b. 1894, followed a different path, training as a medical doctor at the University of Liverpool and working as a medical missionary in India.

Miss Rutherford:

My family have lived around this area since around 1898. My father [Charles Henry Rutherford, 1858-1930] was a solicitor, and I think his father was a timber merchant. My parents were cousins and both of them came from very large families, ten on each side I believe. When they got married, they started in Marmion Road, then they moved to Bentley Road, and I was born there in 1900. They came here to Parkfield Road in 1910.

I started off at a private school in Croxteth Road run by a Mrs. Barrow, a very good school called Melrose. I had three sisters and a brother, who died when he was only two. He was the youngest, then came me and my twin sister. We girls all went to Melrose, then when we got to about 13, we went away to boarding school, to Colwyn Bay [probably Penrhos College].

When we were children we hardly ever went in the Lane. We had telephones, and they used to deliver the goods. We would just go with a nurse or governess once a month with the book to pay the bills. But we used the Park, and used to play tennis a terrific lot at the Mersey Bowmen.

Just about the time I finished with school, it was the end of WW1. My eldest sister and her age group did war work, she joined the V.A.D. (Voluntary Aid Detachment). My second sister just stayed at home. But at that point, 1921, my father became Lord Mayor of Liverpool. We would deputise occasionally for our mother, and two or three times we had our own bits to do. For instance, if you were interested in the Child Welfare Association, then one of us would go along to its Fair instead of the Lady Mayoress.

There were very good shops in Bold Street in those days. There was one particular one called Woolrights. They sold underclothes as well as dresses. But all the people behind the counter were men, and so you bought your combinations from a man! There weren't really any women shop assistants at that time. The First World War brought out women doing all sorts of jobs. Before that they were only domestic servants.

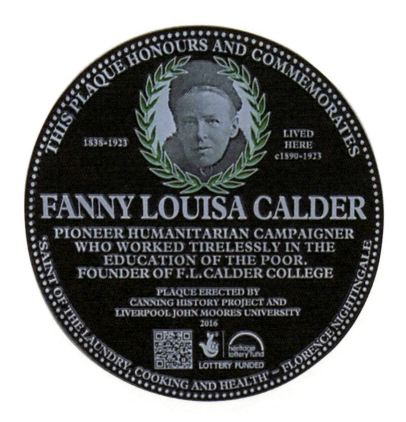

Calder Plaque, 49 Canning Street.

I took one course of cookery in Colquitt Street [F. L. Calder College of Domestic Science, 23 Colquitt Street, bombed in 1941]. They spent the whole time cutting carrots into squares and onions into strips to make a stockpot. I decided it was a waste of strength at the time. I would never want a stockpot. You see, it was before the days of anyone having any idea of not having servants.

The servants all lived in. We had two domestics and they were sisters. There came a point when there was an influenza epidemic. One sister was very ill, and the other wanted to take her home – they lived off Lodge Lane. So, there was I bereft, with Mother an invalid and no servants!

I didn't need to go out to work because we had enough money to live on, but I've done all kinds of jobs in the last fifty years. I was secretary of the Liverpool Needlework Guild for many years. We would collect clothes and distribute them to various charities, and we got a lot of knitting done for us. We used to knit knee rugs for the people in the Turner Memorial Home. But that work is diminishing now, because there isn't the need for clothing that there once was.

The other thing I do is to make jigsaw puzzles. My older sister [Dr. Gladys Rutherford, b. 1894], before she took up medicine, was doing handiwork and started cutting puzzles for the church bazaar. Then she went out to India as a missionary, leaving an order undone, so I took it on. People buy new or secondhand ones and we send them all over the world. We have an annual subscription and a lending library. I had about 100 members at one point.

The area has gone down a lot, and you don't know who you'll meet in the road these days. You hear so much about muggings that I'm afraid to go out alone after dark.

39. Mr. F.J. [Frank John] Camenisch. Solicitor

Mr. Fred Camenisch is the grandson of Mr. John Camenisch (1841-1916) a prominent cotton broker on the Liverpool Cotton Exchange, who originally came from Switzerland and became a British citizen in 1900. A family gravestone in Toxteth Park Cemetery records the names of his grandfather, his grandmother Anna Cecilia (1851-1932), his four aunts Nina (1880-1947), Elsa (1883-1945), Marie (1885-1967), Anna (1888-1944), and his father Frank (1881-1907), who died at the age of 26.

Mr. Camenisch:

I was born in Albert Park and my family lived in Linnet Lane before moving into Ullet Road, backing onto the Park. But my grandfather lived at 8 Aigburth Drive, probably from around 1885. At that time, and until much later, you had a number of famous families, especially Greek families, living there. The Pallis family were Greek: Alexandros (1851-1935) was a director of Ralli Brothers and a great scholar. His son Marco was a well-known climber, led a Himalayan exhibition and was a Buddhist. [Marco Pallis (1895-1989), Buddhist scholar, was also a well-known author whose books include *Peaks and Lamas* (1939) and *The Way and the Mountain* (1960).

The Misses Adam lived in Belem Towers, along with Kielberg, a Dane, who founded United Molasses, and lived in what was known as Valparaiso House. [See *Wikipedia*: Sir Michael Kroyer-Kielberg K.B.E. (1882-1958)]. Then there were Cains, the brewers, the Warings from Waring and Gillow, and the Brunners from Brunner Mond.

There were several sugar firms also living in that area. I remember Fairrie and Tate of Tate and Lyle, who gave the library to Liverpool University. They were very big houses, and unless you had a lot of money and servants you couldn't keep them going. Gradually they were converted into flats. I think the Globes were the last to live on the Drive in a private house. [In 1932, Baron Tobias Globe (1881-1956) who owned a large property business, was living at

32 Aigburth Drive. In 1937 he laid the foundation stone at Greenbank Drive Synagogue].

I went to St. Christopher's in Linnet Lane. But before that I went to Miss Yates' school in Marmion Road. There was Mrs. Cam and Miss Dora Yates, the great expert on gypsy lore. They lived to an incredible age. I stayed at St. Christopher's until 1921 and then went to Sedbergh. My sister went to Sunnyfield in Alexandra Drive and then to St. Winifred's at Eastbourne.

In those days they had trams, and the terminus was Sefton Park Church. They had the usual red trams, and then splendid white trams, which were first class. You paid threepence I think to ride

Horse tram to Pier Head, c.1894.

on them from Croxteth Road to the Pier Head, whereas you paid tuppence on the red. They had blue velvet covers on the seat, and there were marvelous little advertisements in stained glass along the tops of the windows, 'Keating's Powder Kills Bugs' and so on.

It was a penny to Lewis's. Old Mr. Cohen of Lewis's got the City Council to set the fare, so Lewis's became the end of the penny fare and everyone got off there—very useful for the shop! The drivers all stood up the whole time. I used to feel terribly sorry for them. In winter they used to put straw in the front to keep them warm.

8 Aigburth Drive, the residence of cotton merchant John Camenisch.

We used to spend a lot of time in Sefton Park. The gates there are interesting, because they are made from granite pillars. When they opened St. George's Hall, there were two enormous polished granite pillars facing the North Western Hotel. These were known as The Candlesticks. These were taken down, and pieces were used in the building of the entrance gates to the Park.

Once a year the Great Parade of the Liverpool Police Force would be held on the Review Field. A truce would be declared and there would be practically no police left on the streets on that day. All the mounted police with their pennants would march past. As a boy I remember the ground used to shake, because they were big men in

Busy Liverpool tram scene.

those days. A lot of them had big moustaches too. I always used to look forward to that day.

I lived in Ullet Road until I got married in 1937, when we moved out to a flat in Blundellsands. Most of the old families had moved away by then, the big houses were too uneconomical to keep up. But I still use the Lane occasionally for shopping, especially the fish shop.

40. Miss Anne Brocklehurst

Miss Anne Brocklehurst, like Miss Rutherford, devoted her life to charitable work, except during WW2, when she drove an ambulance. She now lives in an apartment at Luchon, 27 Alexandra Drive. I made contact via Francis T. Minoprio, who wrote to KF on May 13, 1981:

Miss Anne Brocklehurst of 27 Alexandra Drive may be able to help you. Her family lived at 20 Alexandra Drive for many years. Her grandmother, Mrs. Calder, lived at 12 Alexandra Drive.

The large 16-room villa of Olinda at 14 Aigburth Drive was built around 1890 for members of the Brocklehurst family, who 'were established in the city of Belém, the centre of the Amazon rubber trade.' The house was named after the city of the same name in Brazil in the northeastern state of Pernambuco.

In addition to trading in rubber, the Brocklehursts and their partners also set up the shipping Red Cross Line connecting Liverpool and the Amazon. [https://warwick.ac.ul/fac/arts/modernlanguages/research/hispanic/hispanicliverpool/stories/villas/olinda.]

Four large greenhouses were part of the original garden layout. Perhaps they included Brazilian orchids and other tropical plants. A Liverpool Horticultural Society display in Sefton Park Palm House in November 1907 included a large display of Cattleya labiata, which originated in Pernambuco.

Miss Anne Brocklehurst:

My maternal grandparents came from America. Grandfather James Calder was in cotton out in South Carolina. He married my grandmother, who was a Southerner, and they came over here during the American Civil War. They landed in Liverpool one Saturday and stayed at the Adelphi. They asked about a church with a good preacher. Canon McNeill [at St. Peter's Church in Church Street] was recommended. So, they went along, and heard him preach a sermon against Americans who were supporting the Southern states. That wasn't what they were expecting to hear! But of course, you can't walk out during a sermon!

I used to go with my mother on Saturday mornings to shop on the Lane. That was very exciting. There was one shop called Truesdale's, a grocer. It had sawdust on the floor, and Mr. Truesdale always wore a cap and a long white apron, with a pencil behind his ear. There was another fascinating shop called Adloms, next door to what is now the launderette. On Saturday mornings we used to get a penny each and go straight to Mr. Adloms. He had a whole shelf of penny toys. Sometimes we would save up and next week buy a tuppenny toy.

The Fire Station on the corner of Lark Lane had a blind horse. I think that was because people thought he wouldn't be frightened at the sight of fire. The harness used to hang on the ceiling, so that it could drop straight down onto the horse for a quick getaway.

Firemen team and engine outside the Ivanhoe Road Fire Station.

Horses and firemen ready to respond to a call.

I always wanted to be a boy. I started off at Miss Yates' school, we all went there. Then I went to Belvedere, while Miss Rhys was the headmistress, and later I went to boarding school in the south for three years.

Then I did a secretarial course for six months, and went into voluntary work, as one did in those days. I am honorary secretary for the Voluntary Society for the Blind, and I go in to the Home for the Blind in Parkfield Road every Friday morning to read to various people.

I learned to drive around 1926; I remember I had an old Morris car. I continued living at home, except during the Second World War, when I was an ambulance driver with Civil Defence.

It's very sad to see this area now, with the disappearance of the families from the big houses and their division into flats. And I'm very worried about all the violence about.

Belvedere School, later the Belvedere Academy.

41. Mrs. Jessie de Larrinaga

The de Larrinagas are one of the old Liverpool Hispanic shipping families, and they still live in a family house in Livingston Drive.

Mrs. de Larrinaga:

My mother was a Miss Moore, belonging to a very old Liverpool family. My father's name was Hands, and they were big hotel owners. I grew up in Gambier Terrace, then the family moved out to Sefton Park Road. After the war the Admiralty requisitioned it, so my mother sold it. It was a lovely house, demolished now.

I went to a school in Croxteth Road called Melrose, run by the Misses Garrett. It was quite well known. When I left there, I was sent abroad.

I met my husband through his sisters, who used to invite me to their parties. He was usually away at boarding school, at Bromsgrove near Birmingham.

My father-in-law Domingo de Larrinaga (1876-1953), lived down in St. Michael's when he was a bachelor. In 1912 he married Minnie de Abreu, who was half German and half Brazilian, and he bought this house. They raised five children here, four girls and one boy, the eldest. He later became my husband.

The top floor was just nurseries. There were six servants and a chauffeur and a washerwoman, plenty of help of course, but then there were a lot of people in the house. They owned the Larrinaga Steamship Company until about six years ago. The family originated in Spain in the Basque country, then it moved to Liverpool and has been here for more than a hundred years.

I first moved to this house at the end of the war. My father-in-law gave it to us after we were bombed out of a house on Aigburth

A garment owned by Minnie de Larrinaga,
now in the collections of National Museums Liverpool.

Drive. This is now the only family house in the district which hasn't been made into flats. And it's a big headache.

I still shop in the Lane. We used to get all our cakes from Stevensons, they were marvelous and would deliver anything you wanted. Deliveries stopped an awful long time ago, just after the war or perhaps during it. People used to be so obliging, but of course it's different now, everything's too much trouble. We always dealt with Tonkiss's too, they used to do all the flowers for the firm.

I think the area has gone down terribly. You can't even get the sidewalks repaired. There are potholes everywhere. I don't think we'll hang on for more than a couple of years. Housing associations spend a lot of money on the property, but then they often put the wrong type in. I don't know anybody around here now. All my friends have moved away, and a lot have gone to Cheshire. We have a nice place in Wales, but we had to stay here because of the firm.

Comment by Geoff Edwards in 2019:

I used to deliver the papers to the Larrinagas at 9 Livingston Drive. On a Friday, I also delivered their monogrammed cigarettes. I went to the front door and gave them to a housekeeper. I never met the family.

When Mrs. Larrinaga took her dog for a run in the park, she would drive slowly along behind it.

M.V. Ramon de Larrinaga, a member of the family fleet.

42. Miss Doris Forster.
Governess and voluntary Social Worker

Miss Forster, born in 1893, is one of the best-known older members of the community. At first, she had to struggle with her father, who wanted his daughters to stay home and 'do nothing'. In addition to her teaching and social work, she was the first Woman Elder of Sefton Park Presbyterian Church, and was responsible for organising its centenary celebrations in 1979. The church, which had once seated about 900 people, was pulled down in 1980.

Miss Forster: My Father and Me

I'm 87 and I've lived in this district all my life. I've had quite an interesting life, though I've never had what you would call a career. I was born into a middle-class family with a father who was rather stern. We lived on the Aigburth Road just opposite the Sefton Park Assembly Rooms. That was a beautiful old Victorian building. We had a day nursery and a night nursery. It was like being in the country, because the trees still ran right along the Aigburth Road.

Dr. John Watson, also famed as author Ian Maclaren.

I remember the first electric trams running into town from Garston. Before that there were horse trams. Every morning we would go to the window and watch the horses being changed. The drivers got to know us and they would never go past without taking off the tall beaver hats they wore then and waving them to us. It was great fun.

When we were children, we went to Stevenson's every Saturday morning and were allowed to choose our own cake for Sunday. (During the week, we had bread and butter with jam.) My favourite was slices with pink and white icing. They still have them.

My father was a chemical merchant, and he died in 1927. He was invited by the ICI to join them, but he was an individualist and hated the idea of being under anybody. His firm was Besson & Vechter. Father and Mother both came from Northumberland. We are supposed to be descendants of the Forsters of Bamburgh Castle in Northumberland.

I had a governess, but in those days, you know I don't think they were awfully good. I didn't go to school until I was 10. She hadn't taught me a word of French, and not much arithmetic. When I first went to school, I remember getting 2½ out of 50 for it.

My father thought that daughters ought not to do anything. It was terrible! You went to boarding school—I went to one in Birkdale and my sisters went to Harrogate. When I left boarding school, I was expected just to stay at home. I had three older sisters and we had three maids, so there was nothing to do.

Last horse bus on Aigburth Road.

I stuck a year of it, but I was so miserable that I went to my father and said, 'Father, I must talk to you. I'm very unhappy and want to do something. You've educated me and now I'm doing nothing!' He said 'I don't understand you. You've got a lovely home and companionship. Why can't you help your mother?' So, I just said 'There's nothing for me to do.'

Then he asked me what I wanted to do, so I said I'd love to teach. He let me go and talk to my old headmistress. She suggested I come back to school, take the Senior Oxford examination, and then take the Froebel training course. So, I did.

Interrupted by WW1 and Breakdown

I had just started on my teaching course in 1914 when I was 21. Then the school received an appeal from the Lord Mayor. He wanted anyone who didn't have to study in order to prepare to earn their livelihood to give it up and go into the business world so that men could be released for the Front. This was a terrible decision for me, but I had three brothers and the eldest one was out at the Front by then, so I felt I ought to do something.

Of all places I was sent to a firm of auditors. Flung into this huge office with about ten men and only one other woman, who was the boss's secretary. I lived in Linnet Lane and I used to cycle home and back for lunch, then home in the evening. Then I was asked to do extra auditing for various voluntary organisations. I didn't dare tell my parents. I'd go upstairs at about ten o'clock and then work for a couple of hours. But that was too much for me, I got thinner and thinner.

I went on until I just collapsed and had to have two operations. I had operation shock after each, then I had a proper breakdown. In those days it was considered something to be looked down upon. My mother did nothing but call in the local doctor, who said 'Just give her a rest in bed.' I was nearly beside myself, and was like that for nearly five years. After the first year my father heard of a specialist in Rodney Street. He used hypnosis. I was with him for five years and he cured me.

Teaching and Community Work at Last

When I was through that, I was too old to go on with my training, yet I still wanted to teach young children. I heard of someone in Rodney Street who wanted a governess for his daughter, so I went along and got the job. And for 10 years until 1939 I was passed on from one family to another. In the meantime, I had also done a lot of church work with Sefton Park Presbyterian Church, which has just been pulled down.

During WW2 I started a canteen in the church for the Pioneer Corps. For 19 years I was chairman of the Union of Youth Clubs in Liverpool. I received a Long Service medal for that from some Duchess, and later I was presented to the Queen Mother. Then when I finished up with the young people 22 years ago, I started a club for lonely and elderly people in the district, and ran that for 21 years.

I was here in Alexandra Drive when we had that bombing for eight days in 1940. We had the cellar strengthened, and two places made where my brother and I could lie down. I could read a letter by the light of the fires in the town. We had our front door blasted up the stairs one night with the impact from two direct hits on houses in Ullet Road.

It's Where I Belong

I don't go out much now because I'm arthritic, and I'm finding old age rather trying. I've never wanted to move out of this area because I feel it's where I belong.

Appendix: In 1977 Miss Doris Forster gave an address to the Women's Guild at her church. It was later published as 'Memories,' a pamphlet describing her recollections of the famous minister Dr. John Watson:

I started my church life in Sefton Park Presbyterian Church in 1897, when I was four years old. The church was built in the 1870s and held over 900 people. It contained a back gallery overlooking the main seating area, flanked by two transepts with beautiful Burne-Jones windows and galleries above. I can remember climbing the stairs and entering our pew. I was completely bewildered by the number of people.

The tram terminus was at Brompton Avenue and the conductors, who used to call out the stops, referred to the Brompton Avenue stop as "Dr. Watson's Church."

I also remember my father discussing the sermon during our Sunday dinner, knife poised in the air, while he expatiated on a particular point in the sermon, till my mother called from the other end of the table to get on with the carving!

Stained glass windows designs after Edward Burne-Jones.

43. The Family of Frank Charles Minoprio: Two Generations on the Liverpool Cotton Market

Some time in the early 1980s, in response to a prior letter, I received a hand-written, undated page of notes on the history of the Minoprio family. The page was written in pencil. Its author was the distinguished architect and planning consultant Sir Anthony Minoprio (1900-1988). His address on printed notepaper was 52 Campden Hill Court, W 8. in Kensington, London. Here is a transcript.

The First Three Generations

Francesco Minoprio, the first M. in our family line, was born in Pavia, N. Italy in 1754. His son Vincent, a merchant, moved to Frankfurt-am-Main in 1877. His grandson Franz Carl Anton (1838-93) married Marie Bertha Klotz (1830-1943) in 1869 and came to Liverpool, where they had nine children.

They lived first at the Tower House, Belvidere Road and later in Livingston Drive, Sefton Park, at Grosvenor House and at Livingstone House. FCAM was on the Liverpool cotton market and acquired British nationality in 1870.

Frank Charles Minoprio:

Mr. Frank Charles Minoprio.

Frank Charles was his oldest son, born 1870, educated first at Parkfield School and later at Southport. Entered the cotton business in Liverpool about 1890 and married Leila Calder (1872-1914) in 1899, living first in Cheltenham Avenue, then at 23 Grove Park, later at 28 Alexandra Drive.

Liverpool Exchange postcard, c. 1905.

They had five children between 1900 and 1914, when Leila died. The children went first to Miss Katie Yates' dame-school in Lark Lane, after which the boys went to St. Christopher's, the school in Belvidere Road run by the Misses Smith. Later the two boys went to Harrow, the two girls to --- [blank].

In 1919 FCM married again, to Rachel Mann, and in the next twenty years had four more children, two boys and two girls.

In 1924 the family moved to Avening Court, Glos, FCM having retired from the Liverpool cotton business in 1920. He had his own firm in Old Hall Street with three branch offices in America. His many interests included pigeons, dogs, gardening, horses, cattle, greyhounds, hackneys, stamps, ...[illegible] and old books on pigeons.

In 1916 he built Haulfryn, a holiday house at Abersoch, Gwynedd, which is still used by his large family.

Sir Anthony Minoprio.

Liverpool Cotton Exchange, designed by Matear and Simon, 1905-6. The front was demolished in 1967, 'an unforgivable act of vandalism' according to Joseph Sharples (*Liverpool*, p.159)

INSTITUTIONS

44. St. Michael-in-the-Hamlet School
Mr. Griffiths, Headmaster.

Perhaps the most influential institution within the area has been St. Michael's School, since for almost a century this has been where the majority started, and for a long time also finished, their formal education. Founded in 1889 as a Board school, its motto 'Service before Self' must have seemed particularly appropriate for children who were mostly destined to go into domestic service or to work in shops. Over the brick entrance gateway of the school is the inscription 'Toxteth Park Board Offices 1889', recalling the older name of this area.

The school takes pupils from the area between the Dingle and Aigburth Vale. The original building still houses the junior school, and until recently the outside toilets were still being used. In the '70s a new building was erected for the Infant School, but plans to begin on a new building for the Juniors were axed with the collapse of the Heath government.

The Headmasters of the school have tended to stay for very long periods. The first Headmaster, Mr. Edwin Horsfield M.A., served from 1890 until 1920, and his successor, Mr. William Scott, who built up the musical life of the school, continued until 1933. The present Headmaster, Mr. Griffiths, came to the school ten years ago and regards this as 'a very interesting area of the city'. The roll has fallen from 330 to 260 over the last ten years, a smaller fall than in other areas of the city.

Mr. Griffiths comments:

The most significant change in my decade at the school is the increase of one-parent families. It's almost an even chance now that when we admit a youngster the mother will mention that there's been a marital breakdown. We're aware of particular children needing a lot of pastoral care, but other children seem to become stronger in coping with their family difficulties.

Football team at St. Michael's, 1977. Popular coach Mr. Crewe is left and principal Mr. Griffiths is on the right. The tower of St. Michael-in-the-Hamlet Church is in the centre. David Webb: 'We were the A-Team.' *(Top Row)*: Dave Webb, Ray Roberts, Neil Turner, Stephen Bird, Stephen Mahoney, Peter Usher, Paul Kyffin. *(Front Row)*: Neil Grace, Julian Rimmer, Alan Brash, Jeff Ablett.

The other development is the shift of families here from Liverpool 8. To them it's a bit nearer the country, and they're proud of having moved up a little bit in the world. There's the Park, good shopping on the Lane and in Aigburth Road, and the railway is convenient for town. A good percentage of the people who have grown up in the neighbourhood consider themselves as being superior to the inner city and they like to refer to the area as Aigburth rather than St. Michael's.

Pre-war and post-war quite a lot of this neighbourhood were associated with the sea or the docks. What I notice now is that we have lots of mums who are involved in part-time jobs in old people's homes, university hostels, and so on. They tend to work 9 to 3:30 or perhaps three mornings a week. And unemployment keeps driving families away. There's some emigration too: in the last few months I've lost two families to South Africa and someone else is going to Canada.

45. St. Charles Catholic Primary School
   Mr. J.F.A. Roderick, Headmaster

St. Charles is a voluntary aided Roman Catholic primary school which opened in March 1896 in a small building on the south side of Aigburth Road. Originally, it had three teachers and sixty pupils, and its current roll stands at 247. Miss McKenna, who joined the school as a probationary teacher in 1941, was headmistress from 1955-1980, when she was succeeded by Mr. J.F.A. Roderick. New buildings were opened in 1974-76 and the old school is now used as a youth club.

Anthony and Rita Cooney outside 17 Hadassah Grove. Mrs. Cooney was a popular teacher at St. Charles School. Kin Hau remembers helping with their garden. TW

Mr. Roderick explains:

Originally Aigburth was a middle-class area. Our intake now is fairly mixed. We have quite a big turnover. Some are families moving from town to here, and from here out to Runcorn. We also have a reception area for children in care, and they tend to stay a fairly short time.

This has always been quite a popular school, with people trying to get in from other catchment areas. Strictly speaking we cover the parish of St. Charles and St. Thomas More, and St. Finbar's takes Dingle children. The way the children behave could be classed as suburban rather than inner city. We're not much bothered by graffiti, but we do have regular break-ins. I think school uniform helps to give it the aura of a suburban school as well.

Anthony Cooney:

My father's mother and father came from the Dingle. They've been in Liverpool for about three generations. My father was a foreman at South End Mills in the Dingle, and I grew up in Garston. My father and his brother used to talk about adventures on the Cast Iron Shore (Cazzy) when they were boys. When I was small, the country started at the end of Garston Village.

A class at St. Charles School, c. 1951-2. Jimmy Archondopoulos is 2nd from left in row 2 from above, and Tom Powell is 2nd from right in the same row.

46. Shorefields Community Comprehensive School. Mrs. E. M. Jellis, Principal.

This large comprehensive school was created in September 1973 by amalgamating four existing schools, Dingle Vale Senior Girls' and Senior Boys' Schools, Wellington Road Council School, and Toxteth Technical Institute. It has now taken over the expanded site and buildings of the Dingle Vale Schools, and the large red brick building of the former Technical Institute now houses their Craft Department. Log Books and other records of the four earlier schools are now deposited at Shorefields.

Before Shorefields: Toxteth Technical Institute

The Toxteth Technical Institute was a trade preparatory school which ran two-year courses for boys prior to their going into apprenticeships. Instruction was given in drawing, practical science, mathematics, workshop practice and physical education.

Shorefields Community Comprehensive School.

Wellington Road Council School

Wellington Road Council School opened in August 1920 as a mixed school taking children from the third to the sixth Standard. Its initial roll was 333. Poverty, unemployment and poor health hit this school particularly hard during the Second World War, many children were evacuated to Winsford and elsewhere, and an attempt was made to run a Home Instruction Scheme based on small groups in twelve private houses. This had to be suspended because of a lack of coal to heat the rooms.

During the air raids of 1941 the school was used as an Emergency Feeding Centre, and heavy bombing on the night of May 6 left many children homeless.

Dingle Vale Senior Girls' and Senior Boys' Schools

Dingle Vale Senior Girls' and Boys' Schools were opened in November 1938. Although the schools were adjoining, teaching was strictly segregated. They were three-stream, four-form entry with about 350 in each school. The Girls' School Log Book mentions a delayed action bomb dropped in nearby Balkan Street in May 1941.

During the 1960s the school showed great enterprise in introducing German classes for the First and Second Year pupils, not for examination purposes, but to make them more aware of life outside Britain. In alternate years school groups also visited a German holiday camp near Cologne, where they spent time with German boys. In 1964 a group was also taken on a holiday to Italy. From 1965 the school was reorganised and merged with the Girls' School to form a co-educational school with an 8-form entry.

Shorefields and the Challenge of Today

In her 1982 report the Principal Mrs. E. M. Jellis, who has been in charge of the school since it opened in 1973, acknowledges the influence of high unemployment on pupils' behaviour, both inside and outside the school:

Principal Mrs. E.M. Jellis:

There is no doubt that confusion, malaise, and hopelessness increase as both adults and young teenagers feel there is no place for them in the world of work.

The school's major need, in Mrs. Jellis's view, is for better grounds and buildings. Ironically enough, the school fence runs right beside the major works of tree-planting and building currently underway in preparation for the International Garden Festival of 1984.

The Principal comments:

On one side of the school fence is an imaginative project costing millions of pounds, and on our side is an inadequate football pitch, frequently waterlogged, narrow paths knee-high in weeds, and the remains of a former pre-fab building. Our priorities in the city do not appear to include a pleasant environment for the children who go to an inner-city school.

Dingle Vale combined dancing class, 1960.

47. Aigburth Vale Comprehensive School
Mrs. Collins, Headmistress

Aigburth Vale School has a proud history as the first public girls' grammar school to open in Liverpool. When it began in July 1908 there were 70 girls and 10 members of staff. 75 years later there are 700 girls and 42 teachers. The present Headmistress, Mrs. Collins, is only the fourth in the history of the school. She comments:

We've stayed comparatively small for a comprehensive because it wasn't convenient geographically to link up with any other school. And we still have a number of teachers here from the time when it was a grammar school. I think they maintained the standard and extended what the school did before, rather than restricting it. They went to enormous lengths to ensure that the new courses in art, cookery, needlework and core subjects were just right, and the girls are doing very well.

In our A level stream, some go on to university, and an increasing number are going into nursing. A lot go into insurance, some adventurous ones go into journalism, and a couple have recently joined the forces as officers. Music and art are also special strengths of the school. In 1979 the Scottish Opera came here with an opera specially written for schools' performance. They brought their principal singers, coached the girls here for just three days, and then put the performance on. It was a great success.

Aigburth Vale Comprehensive School in early days as a grammar school.

48. Sefton Park Branch, Liverpool Public Library
Mrs. Owen, Librarian.

The Sefton Park Branch Library was first opened in 1897 in the local Board offices in Lark Lane. In 1911 it transferred around the corner to its present site, a Carnegie building designed by Thomas Shelmerdine in Tudor Revival style with a garden at the front. The shelves were open access, which was innovative at the time, and the stock comprised 10,000 books for adults and children.

The librarian, Mrs. Owen, comments:

We now have a stock of 50,000 books and a total readership of 174, 258. The membership is mobile, and tends to shift with the student year. We offer a service on demand to housebound readers, but only about 20 are taking this up at present. Borrowings last month came to 18,073, including periodicals. February is the peak month for borrowing, but there is not much fluctuation.

We have good contact with schools, and interschool quizzes are held throughout the winter. But our main readership is older readers who like popular fiction – romantic, detective and western, with the occasional request for a new book. We find there is a great deal of rereading of biographies and other books previously borrowed.

If you compare this branch with Wavertree, then you find there is a smaller issue there, but because there are more retired professionals and students, they dictate a more academic type of collection. Garston is quite close to our pattern, and Allerton is completely different, with a very heavy demand for new books.

Quite a proportion of our readers come from the Dingle. There has been a slow shrinkage in borrowing over the last ten years, but possibly a slight increase in the children's borrowing. We also have many readers from flatland, and the young marrieds from the

Fulwood estate. Most popular authors are Catherine Cookson, Agatha Christie and Van Slyke. Enid Blyton seems to be declining in popularity for children, and there's quite a demand for Dr. Who, Tintin and Asterix.

Comment by Margaret McDermott in 2019:

I worked in Sefton Park Library for a few years in the late sixties. There were still quite a few very posh older ladies living there. One sent her housekeeper to get her books, another would only ever have new ones. It wasn't unusual to find bank notes used as bookmarks, I found a fiver once. The most unusual bookmark was a bacon rasher.

Sefton Park Public Library. KF

Judy Murphy: 'Around 1950, St. Michael's School used to take classes to the library once a week. We would each pick a book and either renew or return it the following week. We would walk in a crocodile from school and back. When I went, Enid Blyton was a favourite!'

Paul Banks: 'You had a little card with your name on it. Surname first, then first name. We used to laugh at my best mate's card because it read ' Byrne Keith.' You would hand over your card, they'd insert a marker and stamp the book. I loved the walk to 'Sevvy Park Lib Lab.'

49. Post Office and Sorting Office

The Sorting Office in Little Parkfield Road was opened in July 1905, and the Crown Post Office in Lark Lane also opened around this time. Both are still in service, although sixteen years ago the Lark Lane office was transferred to private hands and became a Sub-Post Office. It still plays a vital part in the life of the street, since it is one of the places that is used regularly by everyone.

Sian Poynton:

My granddad Albert Poynton moved his family from Wales and took over the P.O. in about 1966, and then my dad Paul took it over in about 1984. We walked away (after a hold-up) in about 1995. Loved the time spent living there, in the flat above and then in a house just down Aigburth Road.

Lark Lane Post Office.

50. Police Station and Fire Station

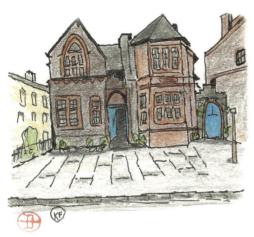

Old Police Station. KF

The Police Station at the Sefton Park end of Lark Lane and the Fire Station at the other end, opening onto Ivanhoe Road, were both built before 1895 and taken over by the Liverpool authorities when the area came within the city boundaries in that year. The Police Station had four large cells, and used to average around sixteen prisoners a month.

In 1976 the local police headquarters moved to Admiral Street, and the building began a new life as the process of converting it into a community centre for the St. Michael's and Lark Lane Community Association got under way.

The Fire Station remained in service with the Liverpool Fire Brigade until 1906. During this period, it was apparently normal practice in fire stations for the harness to be hung from the ceiling on a pulley, and for the collar to be hinged in the middle. When the bells sounded, the stable doors would be released automatically and the horse would be trained to trot out and stand waiting underneath the harness. The aim was to get out of the station in thirty seconds. The fire engines themselves stood at various escape stations out on the street, and one was stationed at the junction of Lark Lane and Aigburth Road, conveniently near the policeman on point duty.

After 1906 the building was used as a Police Ambulance Station, and the yard premises became the Mounted Police Sick Quarters. During the Second World War, however, it once again came into use as an Auxiliary Fire Station, and was occasionally used to house spare appliances for the central headquarters at Hatton Gardens.

51. Telephone Exchange

A telephone exchange was first opened in the area by the Lancashire and Cheshire Telephone Co. Ltd., around 1887. This became part of the National Telephone Company in 1889, and was taken over by the Post Office in 1912. From 1893 onwards it was at No. 25, and later at Nos. 25-27 Siddeley Street, where Mrs. Mary Dolan was the manageress. By 1899 there were 238 lines, and the telephone directory listed two public call offices at the cabbie stations at either end of the Lane. (*The 1899 directory is included in the Appendix.*)

In 1924 a new manual exchange was opened at 38 Alexandra Drive. In 1942 a new automatic exchange was opened in a new building behind the old manual exchange. It closed in 1952 and was demolished in 1975 to make way for an extension to the auto exchange. By 1979 there were 7893 lines.

The development of the telephone service was vital to the shopkeepers of the Lane, since orders were regularly rung through from the big houses. In a wider sense, the existence of a Lark Lane telephone exchange, along with a Lark Lane Post Office, must have helped to increase the sense of independent identity of the area.

52. Churches

Exploring the history of early schools and religious groups in the area takes us back to the early decades of the 17th century. There are important links to New England history, as well as to the history of clock and watchmaking in the Preston and Liverpool area.

Richard Mather (1596-1669) was a teacher and pastor who ran a school in Toxteth Park from 1611. In 1618 he studied at Brasenose College in Oxford, and then preached at what is now known as the Ancient Chapel of Toxteth on Park Road. The first four leasehold farms were also being established around this time—Jericho, the Three Sixes, Parr's, and Rimmer's.

Under the influence of a local member of the Aspinwall family of Toxteth Park, Mather became a Puritan (a nickname given to those who wished to 'purify' the rituals of the established Church of England). This was a time of religious persecution and 'silencing'

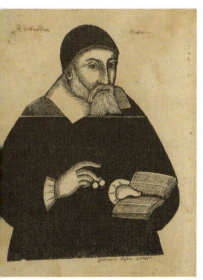

Left: Woodcut of Richard Mather by Boston printer John Foster, c.1670. This is the earliest surviving portrait woodcut in New England. *Right:* Ancient Chapel of Toxteth, Park Road, 1900.

of any who preached dissent. However, for 22 years, between 1611-1633, Mather continued to teach and preach in the Liverpool area (one distinguished pupil was astronomer Jeremiah Horrocks). The Aspinwall family also established a successful clock and watchmaking business in the area. Works by Thomas and Samuel Aspinwall are now treasured possessions of the Merseyside Museums.

Emigration to Boston, Massachusetts

Meanwhile, Richard's fellow pastor John Robinson (1576-1625) moved first from Norwich to Leiden in Holland, and then encouraged his flock to emigrate on the *Mayflower* in 1620. In 1633-1634, after enduring persecution by the Archbishop of York, Richard Mather also decided to emigrate to New England. He sailed with his family from Bristol to Boston, Massachusetts on the ship *James* in 1635.

As pastor in Dorchester, he quickly became a key figure in the religious, educational and publishing life of the new colony. When Harvard College was set up, Mather joined its Board of Overseers and remained a member from 1642 until his death in 1669. His four sons went on to establish the distinguished Mather line of scholars and pastors in the New World.

The Ancient Chapel of Toxteth later became a Unitarian chapel, supported by the Rathbone and Holt families and others. Elfreda Cotton, née Moore, whose mother was Alice Rathbone, remembers growing up at 1 Fulwood Park and attending the chapel. (See above, p. 8).

Before the Sefton Park and Lark Lane area was developed in the 1870s, other churches served the district. The first was St. Michael-in-the-Hamlet Church in St. Michael's Church Road, which was built in 1815. An iron foundry engineer, Mr. John Cragg, was closely involved with its construction, and its frame was made of cast iron. The development of the Princes Park area in the 1840s led to the construction of St. Paul's Church at the bottom of Belvidere Road in 1848.

St. Paul's Church long continued to be a fashionable middle-class church and it also ran church schools in Earnest Street. The 1883 report listed 275 infants and junior school roll of 262 girls and 240 boys. [St. Paul's Church was demolished in the 1970s].

1871 saw the opening of the church most closely associated with Lark Lane, Christ Church. It was built in the decorated Gothic style and cost around £20,000. It could seat 800, and its size reflects the extent of the church-going population at this time.

1879 marked the opening of the Presbyterian church of Sefton Park on Ullet Road. It could seat 900, and there was a waiting list for family pews. The Greek Orthodox Church of St. Nicholas and the Synagogue on Princes Road both opened in the 1870s. The 1890s saw the building of the Unitarian Church on Ullet Road, and the Roman Catholic St. Charles Church on Aigburth Road opened in 1900, replacing an earlier cast iron church.

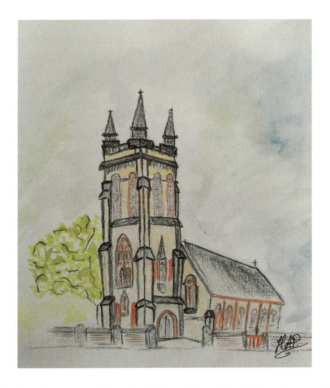

St. Charles Borromeo Church, Aigburth Road by Helena Paxton, 2020.

53. Sefton Park. Sefton Park and Community Life

Since Sefton Park opened in 1872, it has provided the main focus of active and passive leisure activities in the area. In the Liverpool Review of June 1890, the city surveyor of the time was reported as having told a parliamentary committee that the sale of the land for the Park had proved 'A Very Good Thing for Lord Sefton'. Whereas the agricultural value of the land was reckoned at around £350, the sum £250,000 that Lord Sefton had received for it from the Corporation would, if invested at 4%, give an annual return of £10,000. The article went on to condemn this vast enrichment of a single nobleman at the expense of the working masses of the city.

However dearly bought, the Park certainly rapidly became much loved and much used by those same working masses. The Mersey Bowmen opened tennis courts. The Sefton Cricket Club moved its base to the Park, and those who could afford to rode their horses along the Jockey Sands. Everyone could skate on the Lake in severe winters and roam the gardens freely. There were regular band concerts, and Punch and Judy shows were staged for children during the long school holidays.

A little over a century old, the Park looks in less good repair. The railings have not been restored since the war, the Palm House, now brilliantly stocked, is once again in need of restoration, many elms have been felled after succumbing to Dutch elm's disease, and the pond is badly in need of cleaning. The attractive lodge at the Aigburth Vale entrance has long stood boarded-up. It still remains a beautiful, much-used park, offering fireworks displays on Guy Fawkes Night ("Bommy Night"), Summer fairs, and even a keep-fit course. In recent years it has also provided a setting for pop and rock concerts, and its perimeter is now permanently dotted with perspiring joggers.

On the Lane itself, organised leisure activities for all ages now cluster round the Community Centre, which has taken over the role previously played by the Institute building belonging to Christ Church.

The pubs continue to appeal to a mixed age group, while the wine bar and the restaurants cater primarily for the varied groups within the new community. Bingo down on the Aigburth Road is a regular rendezvous, especially for older women, the Sefton Park branch library remains popular, and the Day Centre at the bottom of the Lane is the main meeting place for elderly residents.

Part of the secret of the Lane's continuing vitality lies in the fact that it is both a working community and a leisure community, each supporting the other.

After a Majorettes practice. Mary Ann Archondopoulos with her mother Sarah Benjamin and daughters Lorna (2) and Lisa (6). Steve Archondopoulos, Mary Ann's husband, was born and grew up at 24 Lark Lane, where his parents owned a fish shop and a fruit and vegetable shop. TW

. . . .

The 1980s text of People of the Lane ended here. The next three sections date from 2019-2020, when work on the project resumed after a 40-year interval.

. . . .

III | GROWING UP AROUND THE LANE, 1940-1980

Lunch break at Lucknow Garage. Hayden Langley, Christine Armstrong and Mark Nugent. TW. *Right:* Details of pictorial map, Dave Turton, 2020.

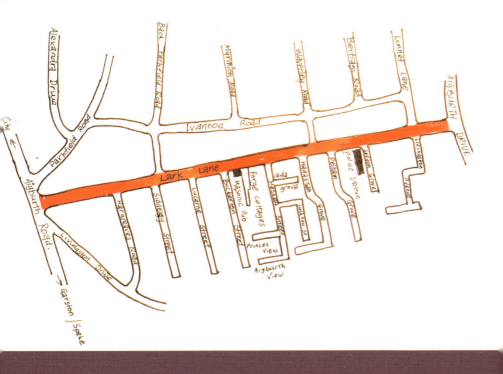

STORIES FROM TEN STREETS

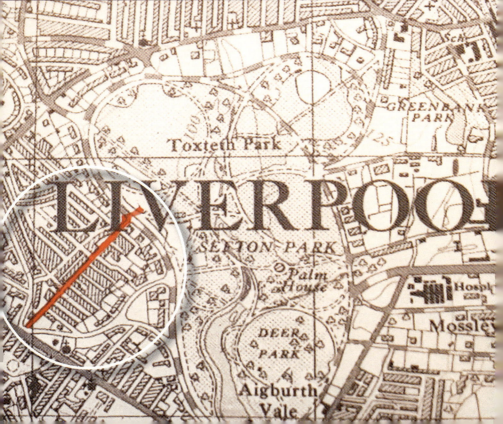

III | GROWING UP AROUND THE LANE

Childhood Memories

In December 2019 I posted this message on the Facebook page People from around Lark Lane:

Here's an invitation to Lark Laners born between 1950 and 1975 (later changed to 1940-1980) to contribute to the interview-based book *People of the Lane*.

1. Your name and year you were born.
2. What street or streets did you live in between birth and age of 15?
3. Childhood memories (ages 4-15)
    i. Food - In Family Kitchens
    ii. Games - in the Street and the Park
    iii. Healthy and Sick - At the Doctor's
    iv. Shopping
        At the Butcher's
        At the Sweet Shop
        Other Shops
    v. Schools and Libraries
    vi. My First Job

The stories that follow are the result of online conversations and question and answer sessions that have unfolded over the past year. This is a wonderfully interactive way to make a book, with contributors scattered around the world! Thank you, everyone!

STORIES FROM TEN STREETS

Contributors

1. *Bickerton Street* - Keith Draper, Jean Wall, née Batten, Joan Major, née Batten, Dave Turton, Lynn Brown Lawrenson, Michael Smith, Sue O'Hagan

2. *Hesketh Street* - Sharon McGovern, née Costain/Luby

3. *Lark Lane* - Judy Murphy, née Halpin, Carole Rich, née Johnson, Geraldine Kaeo, Kin Hau, Andrew Butterfield

4. *Leda Grove* - Paul Banks, Barrie Carlson, Diane Clark, Keith Draper, John Jones, Kay Jones, Harry Letman, Bev Magee, Kathy Wilkinson

5. *Little Parkfield Road* - Graeme Edwards, Elaine Dutton, Mary Russell, née Willingham, Hazel Partington, née Smith, Wendi Surtees-Smith, Philippa Mulberry, née Smith

6. *Marmion Road* - Marianne Ruscoe

7. *Pelham Grove* - Caroline Oates, Peter Vernon

8. *Princes View* - Paul Banks

9. *Sefton Grove* - Eileen Goncalves, née Powell, Alan C. Powell, Tom Powell, Helena Paxton, née Goncalves, Robert (Bob) Stephen White, Beryl Byrne, née White

10. *Siddeley Street* - Lindsay Rimmer, née Walsh, Lynne Bywater, Marg Hibbert, née Kelly

1. BICKERTON STREET

Keith Draper, b. 1942

Keith has been living in Australia for more than 30 years, but hopes to return to the Lane one day. He was a Scout and helped out in the horse repository.

Keith Draper:

I lived at 55 Bickerton Street, right at the bottom, from 1942 until 1962. I remember the coal man, greengrocery man, the milkman and even the horse-pulled bin cart, which was emptied in the Corporation Yard on the corner of Little Parkfield Road and Lark Lane. Our back door was in Bickerton Street, so the bin men had to go down the back entry to bring out the other people's full bins.

I remember Hogg's Dairy, and McFarlane's bike shop, which later became Wright's cobblers. And a shop run by someone we called Maggie Mare. I used to help out with Thwaite's Dairy delivering milk. A lot of people would bring their jugs, which were filled from a churn. Stevensons was the best bakery around, and we had Cheer's greengrocery shop at the top of Bickerton Street.

My earliest memory of Sefton Park is of being taken there. All along the Jockey Sands, as we called it, there were all sorts of army vehicles, jeeps, tanks, etc., being stored there. It was just after the war. I also remember the day a crane arrived in our street with a big steel ball on it to knock down all the air raid shelters in the middle of the street.

We used to play on the plantation at the bottom of the Lane, and the baker's field around in Livingston Drive. I was a member of the 28th Toxteth Scout Group.

I also used to help out in the horse repository, which belonged to a Mr. Rabinowitz but was run by Billy Owens.

I have been living in Australia for the last 30 years, and now I live in Melbourne. But I hope to return for good one day. I have so many happy memories about the Lane. It has certainly changed from when I lived there.

When the Wall Fell Down

The Larrinaga house at 9 Livingston Drive backed onto the bottom of Bickerton Street, behind a big brick wall. Our house was number 55 Bickerton Street. I remember the wall collapsing around

Cheers.

1952. The *Liverpool Echo* took photos from my bedroom window. It was a very cold and snowy winter. As kids, of course, we would sneak into the Larrinaga's garden! And someone would come out and shout at us and tell us to be gone. They thought we were below them. Such snobbery!

Comment by Joan Major, née Batten:

I was one of the children who climbed over that wall! The Larrinaga's Spanish housekeeper would come out and shout at us in Spanish. We didn't speak Spanish, but we knew what she was saying!

That wall had a special significance. One night our dad (Arthur Batten), and his mate Bob Rivington, painted a liver bird on the wall. They also painted a large egg between its feet. It was so big it could be seen from the Lane. For years nobody knew who had painted it. It was a sad day when that wall came down and we lost our liver bird. The Larrinagas replaced it with a higher wall, presumably hoping it would be too high for us kids to climb!

9 Livingston Drive pre-renovation.

Comment by Jean Wall, née Batten, b. 1943:

I lived off Lark Lane from the 1940s until I got married 20 years later. I remember well going up to the dairy, which was a few doors up the street from us, for milk. You had to take your own jug for the milk, which was sold to you by 'gills'.

Can anyone remember us children in the late forties playing in Bickerton and Lucerne streets with a rope on the streetlights, and playing 'Ollies' in the pavement gutters? We called marbles 'Ollies'. You played against each other by rolling your Ollie in the gutter of the pavement, and your opponent rolled theirs, trying to hit yours. That carried on till the winner managed to hit your opponent's, and then the winner kept the loser's Ollie. We all had bags of glass marbles. The boys always beat us girls!

Arthur Batten (left) and Bob Rivington.

Joan Major, née Batten, b. 1944

Joan's stories revolve around her grandmother Frances Batten (Nin), her Aunty Josie, and her happy schooldays at St. Michael-in-the-Hamlet.

From Lucerne Street to Bickerton Street

I was born in Whiston in 1944, but in 1945 I moved with my parents Arthur and Margaret Batten, and my older sister Jean, to 35 Lucerne Street to live with our grandmother Frances Batten, known as Fanny by most people and called Nin by her grandchildren. She was struggling to cope on her own. Her son Bob McPherson, from her first marriage, had gone away to Canada in his teens, and two of the three sons from her second marriage both died in service in WW2. Luckily, our dad Arthur was in the Army and survived the war. So, he came to lend support to his mum. Nin's daughter, our Aunty Josie, was married to Ralph Halcrow and lived across the street at 28 Lucerne Street.

After a short time, we moved into our own place at 27 Bickerton Street, a two-up two-down end of terrace, and stayed there until number 52, a 3-bedroom house, became available in 1960. We lived there until about 1966.

The Battens were part of a much-extended family living in various houses in the Lark Lane area. There were McPhersons, Halcrows, Whites, and Richardsons, to name just a few. They had been part of the community for many years.

The Telegrams

The woman in the Post Office knew the family well. She remembered that in November 1942 a telegram had come for Frances, reporting her son Billy's death aged 20. Four months later, another telegram came for Frances, reporting her son Ernie's death, aged 25. This time the woman in the Post Office told the telegram boy to deliver the telegram not to Nin at number 35, but to her daughter Josie Halcrow at number 28. A few minutes later, Josie was seen running in the street, holding her head and crying "How do I tell her she has lost another son? How do I tell her?"

Frances was a strong capable woman, and her family loved her. She was a no-nonsense lady with a stern exterior which hid a heart of gold. She was a true Royalist who was proud that her sons had served their King and Country and was always at the forefront of any national celebration: Festival of Britain, Coronation, Royal Weddings, her house would be decorated, and usually she would be dressed up as Britannia.

Frances had a succession of dogs and every one of them was called Gyp. She said that it was an easy way to remember their name.

Frances was very much the matriarch of the family, and her word was usually final. She always wanted to reach 100 so that she could get a telegram from the Queen. On her 90th birthday she was quite ill. Her granddaughter wrote to Buckingham Palace to tell them about her. She received a lovely letter sent on behalf of the Queen, wishing her a happy birthday and mentioning her sons' sacrifices. She died a happy lady in 1976 aged 93, surrounded by her family.

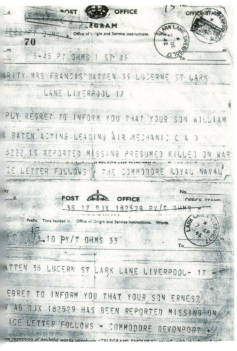

The telegrams.

Frances /Nin as Britannia.

Aunty Josie and the Prince

In December 1984 Prince Charles visited Toxteth and came to see the newly-opened Hesketh Street Housing Cooperative. Josie, then aged 79, was still living at 28 Lucerne Street. As a keen Royalist, she asked Prince Charles for a kiss and he obliged. 'Give us a kiss, Charlie! Grandma puts smacker on her Prince Charming' reported the local paper, along with four photographs of the sweet moment.

Josie asks for a kiss.

My Time at St. Michael-in-the-Hamlet School

There were two schools attended by most children from Lark Lane, St. Michael-in-the-Hamlet and St. Charles RC School. There was always a friendly rivalry between the two. I attended St Michael's School from the age of 5 until the age of 11.

This small school for boys and girls aged 5–11 years was built in 1870, one of the first schools built after the 1870 Education Act. The Infants' section was located near the girls' playground and had a covered area, which contained a sand box. This was covered to provide a stage area for playing. The cover was sometimes removed in the summer. The boys' playground was on the opposite side of the school. These were both small playgrounds.

The Junior classrooms were sectioned off by movable walls, which could be pulled back to allow all the classes to join together for school assemblies. The desks were stepped up on slightly different floor levels, so that all pupils were visible to the teachers. They were located on the 1st floor. The ground floor contained cloakrooms and toilets etc. There was one class for each year, each class usually containing about 40–45 pupils.

School dinners were served at a building a short walk away, and those having dinner were walked there in lines each school day. Likewise, school sports were held some distance away at Jericho Lane, Otterspool, but only for the older children because of the distance to travel.

St. Michael-in-the-Hamlet School. KF

Almost every member of our extended family attended that school, my father, my aunties, uncles and cousins. I loved that school. I was lucky enough to be awarded the annual Permewan Award in 1965. This is given to a girl and boy in their final year for Good Conduct and Service not Self. The normal prize was a watch, but as I already had one, I chose books, including a Bible, which I still have. My cousin Alma Halcrow was a recipient in a previous year.

Pop Davies and His Love of Language

My final year at that school was in Mr. Davies' class. He was known to us all as Pop Davies, and was one of those teachers who makes an impression on you that is with you for life. He introduced us to the beauty of the English Language in all its forms. Some 65 years later I can still recite some of the poems we learned in his class. He taught us how to appreciate English grammar and not to look on it as a chore, but to realise the beauty of it and the influences from other languages such as Latin, French and German. He told us that we should look up a word in the dictionary each day and use it in a sentence. I did this for many years, and still enjoy finding a word 'new' to me.

I know that some of his pupils will have different memories of him, but it is all relative. It was a different time and yes, caning was carried out at that, and every other school. This will of course influence memories of those who were subjected to these punishments, but I think most of his pupils will remember him for the kind, yet strict man he was.

The Waiting Room

When we were kids in the late 40s and early 50s, the Waiting Room was lovely and clean. Each day after school an elderly gentleman used to be there with a small case, which was full of sweets that he gave to us kids. Nothing weird about this, everyone knew him, even the bobby on the zebra crossing on Aigburth Road, he was just a wealthy old man who loved children. It was years later that we discovered that our mums used to give him sweet coupons so he could buy them. They had the coupons and he had the money. I think he lived up in Parkfield Road.

Dave Turton, b. 1955

Dave is the founder of the Facebook page People from around Lark Lane. *He has been living in Germany since the 1990s. Trained as a draughtsman, he enjoys watercolour painting and exhibits regularly.*

My Two Streets

I was born in 46 Bickerton Street in 1955 and lived there till I was five. We then moved to number 1 Hadassah Grove, where I lived until I was nineteen.

I had two older brothers, Brian and Colin, who would be 70 and 71 if they were alive today. I constantly got on their nerves because my Mum used to make them take me everywhere with them. But we did have some great times! I would often go to Sefton Park boating lake with Brian, my eldest brother, and we would sit there fishing for hours and hours. With my other brother Colin, who was really into ornithology, I would go bird-egging to the Park and also to Frodsham on the bus.

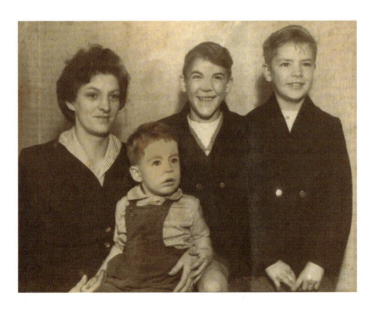

Dolly Turton with her sons Dave (on her knee), Brian and Colin.

Kids on the Lane

We had loads of things to do as kids on the Lane. Playing hide and seek, playing football (all day), getting chased all over by the older kids, stealing apples (seasonal), collecting conkers, roaming all around Sefton Park for hours and hours, carol singing at Christmas. Collecting money on Bonfire Night, building bonfires. Snowball fights, building snowmen, going on bicycle rides sometimes as far as Chester. Camping trips to Wales.

Fishing

I started fishing with my brother Brian when I was about 6 or 7. When I was about 10, I would go along with my friends and quite often alone. We also went fishing in the other local parks, including Greenbank and Princes Park. The most common fish we caught were roach, they were quite small but plentiful. The lake also held quite a lot of carp and tench, which were caught less often.

An inspector would go around and issue day permits. Sometimes we used to fish with one eye on his possible approach and disappear before we had to pay. Also, once he had been around, he seldom returned, so we could then relax. In later years the Council dropped the charges and it was free for a few years.

Comment by Heath Gars

As a small child, my mum Alma Halcrow once went fishing in the boating lake with a friend. When she saw a passing policeman, she immediately stopped and nervously confessed to him that she didn't have a fishing permit.

The policeman carefully inspected her homemade fishing rod, fashioned from a stick, a piece of string and a paperclip. He then winked at her and wished her good luck!

(Turton) Finding the Right Job

My first job after leaving school was as a Junior Draughtsman for an architect in the Liverpool city centre. After 18 months I left and went on the deep-sea trawlers in Lowestoft, South East England.

After nine months there I trained to be a bricklayer, which I am to this day. As for art, I've always been quite good at sketching. About five years ago I enrolled in an evening class for watercolour painting. I took to it really well, and have had quite a few exhibitions in Germany, where I have lived since the 1990s.

David Daniels and the White House

David Daniels lived in the White House at 56 Lark Lane for a few years. I think he was retired from the Army. When I was learning bricklaying in around 1975, my boss and I built a garage for him on the Hadassah Grove side of the house. Now it has been altered and a window added. He hired a small wagon to collect the bricks from the merchants. He drove it himself, as he said he had experience from the Army.

Starting the Facebook Page 'People from around Lark Lane'

I looked in FB for groups in the Lark Lane area, and when I discovered nothing, I decided to start one myself. I now see how useful it is! I had no idea when I started the group that I would manage to make contact with so many old friends and family! It's really amazing that although we have all grown up and some are spread out all over the world, there are times when it's just like we are all sitting together having a cup of tea or a beer like the old days.

Dave Turton, Sefton Park in Winter. Watercolour, 2020.

Lynn Brown Lawrenson, b. 1955

Lynn's memories of games include hide and seek, hopscotch, skipping and stilt walking. Babysitting later earned her 10/- a night. She has been living in Canada since 1989 but keeps in constant touch with family on the Lane.

Lynn Brown Lawrenson:

I was born in 1955 and lived in Bickerton Street with my mom and dad and older brothers, Tommy and Terry. My nan lived in Aigburth View, at the bottom of Hesketh Street, so I would often be around there. We knew every kid on the street, and most of the time we would all play together: hide and seek, hopscotch, skipping (sometimes the mums would turn the rope), froggy froggy. Once my dad made me a pair of stilts, I thought I was so lucky to have them. I would let the other kids have a go of mine, kept us entertained for hours.

Speke Airport.

I remember my mum doing the shopping daily. You could get everything on the Lane: butcher, greengrocer, bakery, *Echo*, sweets, haircut, wool (my mum did a lot of knitting). As I got older, I used to do a lot of babysitting for the kids on the street. One night I was in and out of three houses, watching the kids. I would usually get 10/- a night.

After leaving St. Michael's School I went to Dingle Vale. I left school at 15 and started work as an office junior earning £2.50 a week. I stayed there for about a year, then got a job at the old Liverpool Airport. My wages went up to £12 a week, I really thought I was rich then!

Hesketh Street Housing Association and Working in the Masonic

After I got married, I moved to the Dingle for six years. Then when one side of Bickerton Street and Hesketh Street was about to be pulled down, I joined the Hesketh Street Housing Association.

Prince Charles visits Newland Court, December 12, 1984. 'I asked Prince Charles if I could link him and he said yes,' says Lynn.

I was in from the beginning. We met in Alan Hoyte's small flat. I later moved into one of the new houses built on the site. A lot of the old neighbours moved back, including Elaine Dutton, Pat Georgeson, Adrienne Murphy, Maureen Ashby, Dot Clark and Mary Wareing. After a couple of years Robbie Lewis and his sister Ann moved in. And my mum and dad, Lily and Terry Brown, did a swap with someone and moved in from Bickerton Street.

The houses were visited by Prince Charles on December 12, 1984.

I got a job in the Masonic pub in the Lane, and worked there for just over six years. I loved the pub, as most of the kids I grew up with would come in for a drink.

In 1989 I emigrated to Canada, but I try to get back to Liverpool every year. I still stay on the Lane, as my aunty and cousins still live there. And I still see a lot of my old neighbours and friends. It's like I never left!

Aunty Ada still lives on the Lane, and is 92.

Michael Smith, b. 1959

Michael has lived in the area all his life. His stories revolve around his grandmother Cissy Weston, his granddad William, a train driver, and the Kennerley family, who once lived in the fisherman's cottage at Otterspool. He remembers finding a mouse on the way to school. His career in horticulture grew out of observing his grandmother's passion for climbing roses in her Bickerton Street garden.

Michael Smith:

I was born in 1959 to Joyce and Sydney Smith. We lived at the time in 30 Bickerton Street, and my nan and Granddad William and Etheline Weston lived in number 28.

Old Kennerley Cottage and shore.

I nearly didn't make it, as I got pneumonia when I was three weeks old. Nan had just had a win of £300 in a competition. She threw the money in my cot and said "They can have all that as long as Mike is OK!"

My nan was born Etheline Kennerley. Everyone called her Cissy. She was one of 12. Her grandparents lived in the fisherman's cottage at Otterspool. When she was a schoolgirl, she would walk with an aunty to Park Road to do the shopping for them.

Cissy's working life started off as a shop assistant in Cheers, the greengrocers. She met my grandfather William Weston, a train driver, and married him. They eventually moved into 28 Bickerton

Kennerley cottage, another view.

Street, where she spent most of her life bringing up eight children. As they grew up, they also moved into the street - Aunty Eileen in 26, Joyce in 30, and George in 42.

We moved to Aigburth Vale when I was one. By the time I started school we lived in Roxburgh Ave, off Aigburth Rd. I went to St Michael-in-the-Hamlet. I can remember one day finding a mouse on the way to school, and taking it in to the teacher. She jumped onto a chair in fright and told me to take it outside!

I spent a lot of my school holidays with Nan as Mum worked. I had a few cousins living in Bicky, so we would be taken to the Park. Nan would sit in the bowling green watching Granddad play bowls, while she chatted with her friends and we played in the bushes.

Sometimes my aunties and nan would take a gang of kids to play rounders after school with fruit juice and jam butties. As a special treat we would go to the concert or for a walk round the Palm House, trying to see the oranges, lemons or bananas growing. Happy days growing up!

My secondary school was New Hays. A week after I left school, I started work in the Council's Parks and Gardens Department. My first year was spent in Sefton Park.

Why I Chose Horticulture

I think it was inevitable that I went into horticulture, as my nan loved her back yard. She had a beautiful yellow climbing rose in it, and was always taking cuttings from plants she wanted to grow. I eventually moved to the Council Nursery, where we grew the plants for the parks. We started to do flower shows. I also became the florist for the city. Although my job with the Council ended, I still do the shows with my friend's national collection of Bromeliads. And win prizes!

My Granddad

My granddad was a man of his time. He went to work, and Nan looked after the house and family. He was a train driver. I can just remember him coming in covered in coal dust. I have another memory of watching him walk up Bicky in his suit with his cap on and bowls bag.

Granddad would go for a pint in the Albert and sit with his back to the window, and we kids would bang on the window. Can remember him rolling his cigarette (most people smoked in those days), licking the edge of the paper and rolling it. If he caught me watching, he would wink at me.

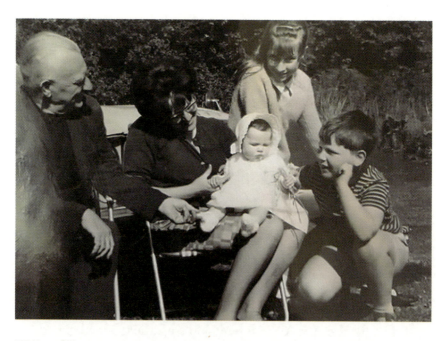

William Weston with his daughter Jean O'Hagan, baby Sue O'Hagan and grandchildren Ann and Michael Smith.

Sue O'Hagan, b. 1967

Sue is a cousin of Michael Smith. Their mothers were sisters. Like Michael, as a child she spent a lot of time at 28 Bickerton with her maternal grandparents, Cissy and William Weston. After St. Michael's she went on to Aigburth Vale High School, and became its last Head Girl.

Sue O'Hagan:

I was born in 1967 and lived on Roxburgh Avenue, opposite the barracks on Aigburth Road. However, I spent a large part of my childhood at 28 Bickerton Street, the home of my nan Cissy Weston. My mum Jean Weston married Brian O'Hagan from 32 Bickerton Street. Even though the street was big, you knew who lived in every house.

My granddad had a tune that he used to call out to me. Wherever I

St. Michael's School, early 1970s. Class of Sue O'Hagan, Teachers Miss Thomas, left, and Mrs. Sidell, right.

was, I would come running back to him for the jelly tot I knew he would have waiting for me. I remember seeing him put the kettle on, on the fireplace. And hearing stories of the seven children and two parents all sitting down to dinner in this tiny little house, with my nan setting out the places by name 'Bill, Jack, George, Fred, Joyce, Eileen, Jean, Jimmy, me (Nan)'.

I remember running through the 'jigger' to Lucerne Street to see Aunty Mary (Evans). And Aunty Tootsie, my nan's friend. I used to buy a 10p mix from Mrs. Robinson at the top of Bickerton Street. Took me ages to decide on the mix of fruit salad and black jacks that I wanted! Other shops: my mum buying live yeast from Stevenson's, and knowing that the house was going to smell lovely of homemade bread later! I remember Mr. Duffy, always had a ruddy complexion and always chatted. A traditional butcher who wrapped your meat in waxed paper. Sawdust on the floor.

Schools

I went to St. Michael's, following in the footsteps of all my family, and I remember all of my teachers. Miss Cowley was the Infants' Headmistress and Mr. Griffiths the Juniors' Headmaster. Miss Thomas was a fashionable lady of the early 70s. I can remember walking behind her in her hot pants on Lark Lane, trying to get my bum to 'swing side to side' like hers did! I went on to Aigburth Vale, where to my delight and my mum and dad's great pride, I ended up as the very last Head Girl. The joy of Facebook is that although I live 'away from home' now, I am in touch with a large number of friends from my Junior and Senior schools. There's just something about 'St. Mike's and 'Aiggy Jail' (our nickname) that stays with us all!

2. HESKETH STREET

Sharon McGovern, née Costain/Luby b. 1960

A Fight for Survival

Sharon was born in March 1960 to local teenagers Sandra and Eddie Costain. Sandra, née Luby, was just 16 when Sharon was born. Her first four years were happy, and include memories of living in a flat at the top of one of the big houses in Parkfield Road. Her dad Eddie Costain worked on the docks and played in a band in the evenings. When she was eighteen months old, her brother Tom was born. Sharon adored him. And she was very close to her maternal grandparents, Janet and Frank Luby, who lived in Aigburth View.

But when she was four, her world collapsed. Her parents split up. Her dad moved out. Her violent and abusive future stepfather, Mick

Hesketh Street sign, 2020.

Garvey, moved into their house in Hesketh Street. From then on, he subjected Sharon to constant sexual abuse and battered her mother. If Sharon dared to speak out, Mick warned her, he would immediately stab her mother to death and then kill her too. Sharon wanted her beloved mother to stay alive. So she kept quiet.

But she also fought back desperately. She was a bright pupil at St. Michael-in-the Hamlet, where her creativity was encouraged by her teachers. She started writing poetry, and had fun with her closest friend Donna Daniels, deciding how to spend their pocket money of 3d a week at Pearson's sweet shop, or piling family laundry onto an old Silver Cross pram and wheeling it up the Lane to the launderette on the corner of Pelham Grove.

When she was nine, her beloved Nan passed away. The following year, her granddad Luby died at sea. Soon afterwards, her family moved away from Lark Lane. Her stepfather continued to abuse her until she ran away and tried to survive on her wits. 'Living in my imagination is how, from the age of four to seventeen, I survived the constant and brutal abuse my stepfather inflicted on me.'

The Pursuit of Justice

As a mature adult, Sharon found the courage to denounce her abuser and pursue justice through the courts. She received strong support from her lifelong friend Donna, her brothers Tom and Phil, and her uncle Gordon Luby. In 2004, a jury trial at Liverpool Crown Court found truck driver and petty gangster, Michael Charles Garvey, 62, guilty on four charges of rape and indecent assault, dating back 40 years. He was sentenced to 13 years in prison and died in Spain six months after his release.

Sharon has dedicated her life to helping others find their own paths from abuse to survival, justice and achievement. She regularly gives inspirational talks to groups of all kinds, including victims/survivors and professional societies.

Sharon:

Throughout my teens suicide was never far from my mind. Who was I? I was never sure - living a double life from the age of four was damaging and destroyed who I should have been. Having my first child David at 19 saved my life. I had someone who NEEDED me! I never felt loved, wanted, or needed before. Three children later, I decided to be who I wanted to be and reinvented myself. Then and only then, could I begin to learn to love me.

I am now happy and at peace. Yes, I still have nightmares and flashbacks, they NEVER leave you. It's learning how to accept that, at 60yrs of age my life is full of love and acceptance of me, knowing the nightmares and flashbacks are the abuser's way of trapping you in the past. We survivors and victims alike have to keep fighting the memories and put them where they belong …in the past.

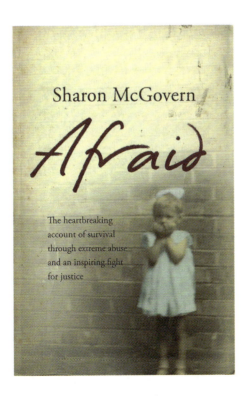

Memoir, 2008. A brave and riveting story.

3. LARK LANE

Judy Murphy, née Halpin, b. 1946

Judy lived first above the family shop at 23/25 Lark Lane, and then at 56 Lark Lane. She has become a keen chronicler of 'the Martin era' on the Lane.

The Martins on the Lane

I was born in 1946 at a private Nursing Home 'Linwood', which was in Parkfield Road. I attended St Michael-in-the-Hamlet School. My grandfather died at an early age, so my grandmother Julia Alexandra Martin was left to bring up their four daughters, and a son James Thomas, (Jim). She decided to set up the two

Martins' Store is on the corner of Siddeley Street.

shops with my mother (Annie Halpin), and Aunty May (Maisie), running the bedding and soft furnishing shop in 25 Lark Lane, and Uncle Jim and Aunty Hilda running the antique shop at 2 Lark Lane. They opened on the Lane around 1947.

We lived above 23/25, which my mother owned, for many years. Then we moved to the White House at 56 Lark Lane and lived there until 1976. Attached was 58, which we also owned. It was a massive stable/garage with a loft room above it. The previous owner was George Charlett. He lived there with his housekeeper and her husband, who also worked in the funeral parlour.

The Antique Business

Uncle Jim had no prior experience in the antique business, but ended up as a well-respected knowledgeable dealer. (As a young man, he was offered a position at Sotheby's in London, but my grandmother would have none of that!)

Hilda and Jim and my grandmother owned and lived at 11 Hargreaves Road. My grandmother bought that house lock, stock and barrel, as it had been Miss Bumfries' Home for Retired Nursing Gentlewomen. At that time, I was only about 10. I can still see in my mind the brass plaque on the front gate with words to that effect!

At Number 2, there was an oval plate glass hanging in the corner window. It said 'Antique and Modern Furniture MARTINS' and the phone number, which was LAR 1798. You could see it as you walked up the Lane. When my Aunt Hilda sold the shop, she smashed the glass, as she said that was the end of the Martin Era. I remember taking photos with my little Brownie 125 camera outside the shop. Some were of my Aunt Hilda and her good friend Olga Casartelli. Olga was the wife of Gino Casartelli of Casartelli Bros, who had the business on the corner of Duke Street in Liverpool City Centre.

After Henderson's horrendous fire in June 1960, the shop sold clothes, shoes, household goods, perfume, in fact practically everything that Henderson's high-class store sold! All purchased at the salvage sale following the fire.

Mrs. Tinne's Silks

Another interesting story: Emily Tinne, wife of a Liverpool doctor, lived at Clayton Lodge in Liverpool 19. Mrs. Tinne was a compulsive buyer of clothes and in fact everything: gloves, tea sets, kitchen equipment, writing paper etc. She also purchased rolls and rolls of material including pure silks, shot velvet, crepe de chine, curtain material etc.

Annie Halpin, née Martin with young Judy Martin, her Aunty May (Maisie) and dog Toby.

After she died, one of her daughters had the handyman/odd job/gardener and his wife (who lived at the little detached house at the bottom of the drive up to the Lodge) liaise with my mother. She would purchase materials and other goods, which would be sold at our shop.

In the late sixties, early seventies, we used to have regular visits from a fellow called Johnny. He worked for Mr. Fish, who had a trendy clothes shop in Carnaby Street, London. Johnny would cause quite a stir in the Lane, as he had long wild hair and would appear in trendy flower power suits with massive flares in material such as Mickey Mouse prints. He would buy rolls of material, pack them in his little mini-van, and have them made into clothes sold in Carnaby Street.

Hilda's Spring Flowers

St George's flag ALWAYS flew outside every 23rd April to celebrate St George's Day. In the spring, Hilda would plant magnificent displays of daffodils, hyacinths and tulips for the shop front window. It became a delightful sight for people walking up the Lane, receiving compliments galore from passersby. She was self-taught as an upholsterer of small items, which she completed to perfection.

Lark Lane was a lovely friendly place to be brought up in.

Comment by Geraldine Kaeo:

I was born and grew up in Siddeley Street. Hilda and Jim had the most beautiful antiques. Hilda was a lovely woman, very kind and patient. And Maisie was my favorite shopkeeper. I thought she looked like a gypsy. She had jet-black hair and always wore gold hoop earrings.

Carole Rich, née Johnson, b. 1947

Carole was born above the shop at 29 Lark Lane and has lived in Newland Court since the 1980s. She remembers her grandmother Nellie Curran's ginger cat would follow her nan up the Lane to Mr. Duffy's, hoping for a tasty treat from the butcher. Joe's Milk Bar in the 1950s was a special favourite with children.

Carole:

I was born Carole Johnson in 1947. My great-granddad David Patrick Walsh came from Belfast. My mum's maiden name was Lily Curran. She met my future dad, Richard Johnson, who came from Wigan, when he was billeted on Linnet Lane during the war. The soldiers were put up in two big houses where Bloomfield Green is now. One house had a direct hit and many soldiers were killed. My dad was lucky because by that time he had been posted to Paris. They married in Christ Church on Linnet Lane in 1945.

When I was growing up, we lived at the back of Bob Norman's shop at 29 Lark Lane. Bob sold hammers, nails, screws, anything for the handyman.

His father was also called Bob. He used to give me a halfpenny to go to Hogg's and get him a pint of milk.

We had five bedrooms and a bathroom. The three main windows above the shop were a lovely big sitting room. The building is now a pub called The Rhubarb. When you walk to the back part of the pub, you enter what was our living room, with the door to the cellar. We used to go up those stairs carrying buckets of coal for the fire.

At that time the building that is now Maranto's, had the baby clinic on the ground floor. My mum used to send me there with a coupon to get free orange juice. The middle floor was used as a youth club, and the top floor was for the Girl Guides. The Scouts were across the road in the old Sunday School building. It's a pizza place now.

My gran, Nellie Curran, had a ginger cat that always sat at the front door. When my gran went up to Jim Duffy the butcher, at 41 Lark Lane, the cat would follow her and wait for a scrap of meat from Jim.

Those were the days when everyone left their doors open.

Joe's Milk Bar

In the 1950s Joe's Milk Bar and Café was where Chy is now. It was run by Mr. and Mrs. Green. They had a daughter named Marion. My Curran uncles (Mum's brothers) all went away to sea. Each time they were home they'd take all their nieces and nephews to

Newland Court, built by the Hesketh Street Housing Cooperative.

Joe's, buy us all kinds of food (especially ice cream soda with ice cream in it) and leave us there for the afternoon. We loved it!

Living in Newland Court

My husband Roy was chairman of the Hesketh Street Housing Association when Newland Court was visited by Prince Charles in December 1984. It opened in February 1983, 37 years ago this month. It took four years in the planning and building, as Alan Hoyte and Lynn Brown Lawrenson have described. Later on, I was maintenance officer for 15 years. It's a close-knit community, and I won't ever move from here.

Picnic in the Park. A birthday celebration by the Rich family and friends. TW

Kin Hau, b. 1962

Kin Hau's parents were a key part of the life of the Lane for 47 years, through their popular chippy and Fish and Chinese General Store. 'We knew everybody,' says Kin Hau happily.

Kin Hau:

I was born in 1962 and grew up on the Lane, went to St. Charles School. Mrs. Cooney was one of my teachers there, and we used to tidy her gardens for her. My parents Mr. Ping On Hau and Mrs. Andrea Hau had the chippy facing Pelham Grove from around 1967 for 22 years.

So, we knew everyone.

They sold that, and later in the 1990s they bought Glendinning's old store at 91 Lark Lane, and ran it for almost 25 years as a fish and Chinese general store. The storefront was always kept full of plants. Stock came from the Flower Market and Fish Market. They worked hard and now miss the Lane.

I must admit I was lucky to have been brought up on the Lane. It was the best place in the world. Great people, and Sefton Park as your garden!

Andrew Butterfield, b. 1965

Sefton Park in the 60s and 70s was the centre of Andrew's childhood world. Football was supported by the local community organisation and sponsorships enabled all young people to participate.

Andrew:

I was born in 1965 and lived on Lark Lane for most of my childhood years and my mother and father owned Butterfield's greengrocers next to the Masonic pub.

I attended at St. Michael-in-the-Hamlet primary school. Sefton Park was my playground, and most of my happiest memories were in the Park. A group of us would spend hours playing football or cricket in the Park. I remember a very close-knit community where you could leave your front door open without any fears. I had so many friends: Ian Tennant, Russell Doswell and Ste Georgeson, to name just a few.

We played football for SMLLCA located in the Old Police Station. We were sponsored by Jim and Jane Baxter, who paid for our new kits. Our manager was Bill Rawlings, ably assisted by his wife Nora. I played from the age of 7 until 18. We were one very successful side, winning league and cup on many occasions. One of our players, Gary Ablett, even went on to represent Liverpool and Everton. We both attended St. Michael-in-the-Hamlet and St. Margaret's, and we were pictured by the *Echo* on opening day.

Butterfield's shop was on the corner of Lark Lane and Bickerton Street.

4. LEDA GROVE

Memories of Leda Grove:

Responses from Facebook

This is a chorus of memories from residents and former residents. Bertie Bell the chimneysweep and his wife Nellie lived in the Grove, Kathy Wilkinson recalls.

Paul Banks:

I lived in Princes View, but always thought Leda Grove looked nice. I think it was the colour of the bricks, and its layout.

One strong memory I have is of a loose brick, of all things. It was on the corner of the back door to the house on the right, just after the white window. It was about 6 bricks up from the floor and had no mortar in it, so you could twist it out. We used to hide "treasure" in the indent (the frog), on the top of the brick and then slide it back in place. When I came back years later and hunted for the brick, I couldn't find it. [See Paul's larger story under Princes View].

Diane Clarke:

My great-grandmother, Mrs. Sweeney, lived there during the war.

(left): Mrs. Mabel Sweeney (née Hodges, born 1883) lived at 6 Leda Grove from around 1918 until her death in 1972. After the death of her husband Patrick in January 1918, she reared their four children Kathleen, Sydney, William and Dorothy. During WWII she worked in the Corporation Yard in Lark Lane, as a street cleaner by day and an air raid warden at night.

Keith Draper:

My friend, Alan Robinson, lived there. Around 1957, when I was still at school, we had a band called 'The Darktown Skiffle Group'. We practiced in Alan's house in Leda Grove – guitars, piano and Richie Starkie (Ringo Starr), on drums. That was before his Beatle days.

John Jones:

We lived in number 2, the smallest house we ever lived in. Two-up, two-down, with a toilet in the yard and a leaky roof. We used to put a storm lamp against the water pipe to stop it freezing.

Kay Jones:

I was born there in 1940. I left in my late 50s and went to Siddeley Street, but my mum still lived there.

Harry Letman:

My dad's brother, Arthur Letman, lived there, around 1952 to 1959, I guess. He and my dad both had allotments by my old school, Dingle Vale.

Bev Magee:

I lived in the next street, Lucknow, and I always played in the Grove with my friends. I used to think how pretty it was and wished I lived there instead of where I lived, facing a garage and a very old brick wall.

Kathy Wilkinson, b.1955:

My nan lived in 12 Hesketh Street, right opposite Leda Grove. Her friend Nellie Bell, lived in the Grove. Her husband was Bertie Bell, the chimney sweep. Bertie also attended most of the weddings for luck.

Leda Grove, 2020.

Leda Grove sign.

5. LITTLE PARKFIELD ROAD

At Dr. Macken's Surgery: Three Memories

Many stories about visits to the doctor can be found on People from around Lark Lane. *These three entries, posted at different times, evoke the complex character of Dr. Macken, the smoke-filled surgery, and the many challenges that were confronted by family doctors. 'Great doc… a man of the people,' says Elaine Dutton.*

Graeme Edwards:

Dr. Macken's was at the corner of Little Parkfield and Lark Lane. The waiting room was always full of smoke, as was his surgery. His wife was the receptionist. Once you got past Mrs. Macken, it was always a good sign!

Despite the smoke, Dr. Macken was a fantastic doctor. I remember his house calls and getting me rushed to hospital with appendicitis. My younger brother Ross tried once to light the fire in the living room, and set fire to his socks. He was taken to Dr. Macken and immediately given special gauze soaked in medication ordered from Mr. Perkins the chemist on the Lane.

Elaine Dutton:

As well as getting you better, Dr. Macken would offer patients a cig if they went to him with a problem and needed to talk. He was also known to give out tips for horses. If you were really ill, it was best to go to morning surgery, as he had had a good drink by the evening surgery. Great doc, lived on the Lane, a man of the people.

Mary Russell, née Willingham:

Remember him well and his big leather chair. He was a real 'family doctor'. I lived in Lucerne Street with Christine Crabtree, Maureen Beckett, Linda Thompson and Lyndsey Walsh. I married Stuart Russell from Siddeley Street.

Three Sisters Remember: A Group History

Hazel Partington, b. 1957
Wendi Surtees-Smith, b. 1960
Philippa Mulberry, b.1965 (all née Smith)

These interwoven stories of three generations start in 1940 and continue into the 1970s. They include stories of the bottle-washing factory that converted to making plastic bottle tops, and memories of the era of the tin bath in the kitchen.

Hazel, Wendi and Philippa:

The story of our family in Little Parkfield Road and around Lark Lane began around June 1940, when Leonard Sidney Smith, his wife Elizabeth Agnes and their four children were evacuated from Jersey as the German Army invaded the Channel Islands.

Len and Lucy with Wendi and Hazel in her first communion dress.

Len Sr. was born in Kent in 1912, and Elizabeth was from the Scotland Road area in Liverpool. When they moved to Liverpool, they were apparently gifted 13 Little Parkfield Road by a benefactor – sadly we don't know who the benefactor was.

Our dad was the eldest child. He was born in December 1930 and named Leonard after his father. As a youngster, Len Jr. worked at some point in the bicycle shop then on the corner of Lark Lane and Little Parkfield. After doing national service in the RAF, he went to work at Dunlop in Speke, where Len Sr. also worked.

Len Jr. was a member of one of the local cycle clubs, and it was here that he met our mum, Lucy Timms. After they married in 1955, Lucy worked as a florist at Tonkiss's on the Lane. She stopped working after having Hazel in 1957, but she used to tell us about going to the docks to do flowers on the cruise liners.

When they first got married, Lucy and Len lived in a flat near to Allerton Road, but it wasn't long before they moved back to Little Parkfield Road, renting from the Hemmings family. They lived in 3 different houses on Little Parkfield. The first house, number 12, was next door to the bottle-washing factory, which was also owned by the Hemmings family. In addition to working at Dunlop's, Dad would supplement the family income by working weekend shifts at the bottle factory. After the factory converted to moulding plastic bottle tops, Dad would work a 24-hour shift over the weekends, keeping the machines topped up with powder to make the tops.

When Hazel was born, Lucy and Len were living in number 12 Little Parkfield, close to our nan and granddad. By the time that Wendi arrived in 1960, they were living in 13a, and by 1965 when Philippa came, the family had moved to Lark Cottage, which was then fronted by a row of terraced houses on Little Parkfield.

Each house that we moved to was an upgrade on the previous one. At number 12, Mum had to cook on a black-leaded grate; 13a was a two-up-two-down with a coal fire in the living room, a gas cooker in the kitchen, an outside toilet and a tin bath in the kitchen. When we moved to Lark Cottage, it felt like a real luxury to have an extra bedroom and a bathroom in the house.

At Lark Cottage

Lark Cottage was originally a coachman's cottage and was next to a stable block. During our childhood, the stables had been converted to garages and workshops, and were later converted to mews flats. Liverpool footballer, Ian Callaghan, used to rent one of the garages to house his car, and it was always very exciting if we saw him bringing his car back after a match.

The Lane, the Park and the Prom

Little Parkfield Road was a great place to grow up. We were near to the Lane, which seemed to have everything we needed, near to Sefton Park, which is still a favourite place for all of us, and near to Otterspool Prom, another favourite place to visit. However, living on Little Parkfield also had a downside—the awful smells that emerged when pigswill was being prepared at Hogg's farm, which was just up the road from our house!

Hazel:

I remember stopping with Wendi at Stansfield's newsagents on the way to St Charles' School to pick up our break-time snacks. Mrs. Stansfield would have our KitKat ready in a little paper bag for us each morning, but Dad, (Len Jr.), and Pop Smith, (Len Sr.), got their papers from the newsagents on the other side of the road. I remember being sent to get 'Len's paper' and being confused when asked if it was for 'Big Len' or 'Little Len', then even more confused to find out that Dad was little Len, even though he was taller than our granddad!

Hazel and Wendi:

As teenagers, we both worked for Mr. Williams at the chemist shop on the Lane. Mr. Williams was a lovely man to work for and we worked with some lovely staff – Lorraine, Claire, Esther, Pam, Irene, Sheila… it was a happy place to work and many laughs were had behind those counters. Mr. Williams was a generous boss and would put money in a box each week to pay for food for the staff at break-time. We would take it in turns to go to Stevenson's to buy sandwiches, pies, cakes, etc.

At the top of the Lane was a shop that sold toys and children's wear. Mum used to put money away there over the year for the Christmas Club, which made life easier for her and was very exciting for her daughters. Mum's usual shopping route took us up one side of the Lane and down the other, calling at Quigley's, Valentine the butcher, the greengrocer on the Lane and the shop on Bickerton Street.

On the corner next door to the Police Station was a haberdashers/wool shop run by two sisters. Mum would refer to them as 'the Bronte sisters' because it had a sign over the front door advertising Bronte wools. They sold wool, buttons, cottons, etc., and provided a sewing service.

Dad loved a potter up and down the Lane. He would take a stroll every day to collect his paper and, once he'd retired, "have a mooch". As the number of eateries on the Lane increased, there was plenty of choice for where to go for a cuppa/spot of lunch/evening meal and you could guarantee he'd bump into someone he knew. A big friend of his was Bobby Guest, an amazing man who was still game to get up on a roof to mend it until well into his old age.

As children it was very exciting to be given empty bottles to take back to the shop on the corner of Little Parkfield and Lark Lane to get the money back on them. Of course, the money was instantly spent in the same shop on sweets!

The Lane provided a mix of community, entertainment and all the other essential things in life for the Smith family, and holds a very special place in all our hearts.

6. MARMION ROAD

Marianne Ruscoe, b. 1969

Marianne is very proud of the heritage of her great-grandparents Edward and Margaret Ruscoe, who moved to Pelham Grove in 1881. Her grandfather Walter was born there, and her father was born in Princes View.

Marianne:

I was born in 1969 and lived in 26 Marmion Road for 26 years with my mother and father, Mary and Eddie Ruscoe, and my older brother and sister. I left in 1994.

I feel very protective of the Lane, it's still my home in my heart. I lived through almost three decades there. It's a place that keeps changing and giving, a very special place where I grew up, and fundamentally made my character.

There was always a famous face on the Lane. I remember seeing The Real Thing all the time in the late '70s strolling up and down the Lane. Liverpool FC after they recorded the Anfield Rap in the recording studios down Hesketh Street. They were all coming out of the Masonic, my dad was in there at the time and he was thrilled to bits to be having a pint with the lads of his team! I remember John Barnes smiling at me as he crossed the road! The Albert and the Masonic were the hub of the community and I was never allowed in any of the pubs, as it wasn't a place for children, I was often told.

There were a lot of generous people around the Lane who would pay you well for running errands for them. I'd have my penny for a guy outside Dunbavin's bookmakers, I made a killing that year! Then I

26 Marmion Road.

Margaret and Annie Ruscoe.

16 Pelham Grove, 2019.

Margaret and Kate Ruscoe.
16 Pelham Grove, c1890.

spent it all in Winny's bag shop on a giant blue corduroy tubular bag I had my eye on! I must admit we were all little rascals, very much each man for himself!

The Ruscoe family had a long heritage on the Lane. Edward and Margaret Ruscoe, my great-grandparents, came to live in 16 Pelham Grove in 1881. Edward Ruscoe died on 9th March 1888 at his home in Pelham Grove, aged 57, after a short illness. His wife Margaret died aged 83 in 1912, still in Pelham Grove. In 1911, six of their children were still living at home and still unmarried, all by then in their 40s. My grandfather Walter was born there.

I have pictures of my Victorian aunts Annie and Margaret seated in their garden at Pelham Grove. They were commercial clerks. They never married. If any of the children saw their aunts on the Lane, they were not allowed to say hello to them!

Aunty Lilly, my father's sister, told me that every Christmas Eve my grandfather Walter, who was married with a young family and struggling financially, would go around to Pelham Grove. He would be given new bed linen and blankets, as well as new outfits, and a toy each for the children. On Christmas Day, all the children would go and visit their aunts and thank them for their gifts.

My grandparents were Alice and Walter Ruscoe. My dad Eddie Ruscoe was born in Princes View in 1916. He was the last of eight brothers and two sisters. Five of them continued to live on there all their lives. I remember that after my dad died in 1995, I'd walk up the Lane and feel sad that none of us Ruscoes lived there anymore. Sometimes I would go for a walk at night and go and look at the family houses and remember all the memories of times gone by.

7. PELHAM GROVE

Peter Vernon, b. 1950

Peter's story focuses on the life of his grandfather George Vernon, who was married in Liverpool in 1921 and ran his own nursery gardening business for the next forty years. Peter would accompany him on Sunday morning visits to water plants in a Larrinaga greenhouse. His parents kept chickens in their garden in Pelham Grove.

Peter:

I was born in 1950 and lived in three houses in Pelham Grove. I lived first at number 3 with my parents and grandparents. Then my parents bought 18 Pelham and we lived there until I was 11. We had chickens and grew veggies also. We never discussed family and their history. If I asked, I was always told 'You don't need to know that'.

Pelham Grove street sign, on the wall of the Albert Hotel.

We then moved to Garston for just over 12 months. The three Mather sisters, great friends of the family, lived at 13 Pelham Grove and were moving, so my parents bought their house. We were there for 6/7 years, then moved to Ullet Road end of Linnet Lane. In the meantime, my grandmother had moved from 3 Pelham and bought 15, which was in flats, and lived on the first floor.

My grandfather George Vernon was born in Bickerton, Cheshire. He was a nursery gardener. Her served in WW1, and I believe he probably arrived in Liverpool just after the end of the war. He married my grandmother in Liverpool in July 1921. She was born in Manchester and served with the Queen Alexandra Medical Corps. I assume they met during their service in the war.

My grandfather had his own gardening business and had some very well-off clients including Miss Forbes-Bell, (she wore a mob cap on her head), the Molyneux-Cohans, and Miss de Larrinaga, whose family owned a steamship company. He rented some land at the rear of the Albert Bowling Green from Cain's, the brewery who owned the Albert, to use for his business growing plants etc. He also had an allotment in Livingston Ave.

Albert Bowling Team. Mr. Vernon is 2nd from the right, and Tom Powell Sr. is 6th.

He was a keen Crown green bowler and was a member of the Albert bowling team who played in competitions.

Miss Larrinaga was a lovely lady with a tragic story. Always dressed in black from the day she was banished from seeing her love, who, I believe, was considered to be unsuitable. I also heard that from that day she never had a man friend. She lived on her own in the big house at the bottom of Ullet Road in later years. I think she ended up in Lourdes hospital, paying privately to live there. My dad used to visit her from time to time.

When I was a youngster, I would walk across Sefton Park on Sunday mornings with my grandfather to water their plants in the greenhouse. Miss Larrinaga's brother had a horse stabled there, and I used to see him riding along the Jockey Sands in Sefton Park. Happy days.

Engineering or Gardening?

My dad Harry Vernon was an engineer who served his time in shipbuilding. He worked at Cammell Lairds and a few others, and also worked at various collieries maintaining winding gear etc.

When my grandfather died in 1962, he still had a good business and employed 2 others. So, my dad thought it a good idea to keep the business going. It did OK for a period, but gradually the people in the big houses died or moved on, and properties were converted to apartments. Others began to look after their own gardens. Eventually my dad went back to engineering at Cammell Lairds and then at smaller businesses. He was still working until he died at 70.

The house at 15 Pelham Grove was left to my dad when my grandmother died. When I got married, we lived in the flat for a few years before moving to Aigburth Vale.

Moving On

I remember Ann Beattie, she used to live at the top of Pelham Grove next to the entry. Before it became a launderette, the shop was called Brooks and was a general store selling bread, cheese, cold meats and tinned foods etc. The manager I knew was Mr. Jack. I used to be an errand boy on the bike making deliveries, including to some of the big houses along Aigburth Drive and Livingston Drive.

After leaving school I started by working in a few clerical jobs, but most of my working life was spent in Sales at Metal Box Speke. When that closed, I worked at a carton printer in Congleton, and finally for a Security printing firm in Runcorn. I retired at 58. Now I live in New Zealand.

Caroline Oates, b. 1969

Caroline is an independent fashion designer and photographer, whose photographs of the Lane and the lake in Sefton Park grace this volume. She is grateful to both parents for encouraging her creativity from her early years.

Caroline at Keith's, 2019.

Caroline:

I was born in December 1969 and grew up in Pelham Grove. I still live there. I knew from when I was six that I wanted to be a dress designer. It's my passion, being creative and helping women of all walks of life. I was lucky because both my parents were really creative. My mum Katherine taught me embroidery when I was only five or six, and my dad taught me about art and drawing.

Then I used to watch all my big sisters – Sue, Ann, Katherine, Shelagh and all their friends - going out dancing to 'Saturday Night Fever'. I loved seeing the clothes they wore. My neighbours Kay, and her daughter Rebecca, who's my age, influenced me too. As I got older, I realised I could go to college and it wasn't just for posh people.

I took a class of sewing at Liverpool City College, and was given a project to design a range of children's wear for British Home Stores. My designs were chosen! I was given a 6-week placement, and during that placement I got loads of experience using jersey fabrics. I still apply that today in my collections.

There were not many jobs in Liverpool at the time, so I decided: 'Nothing to lose, I will create my own job!' I followed Roy Halston, the New York designer, and the clothes that Bianca Jagger wore. And Studio 54.

I decided to invest £3500 in launching my own small business as a fashion designer. I applied to the Prince's Youth Business Trust and had to go through interviews, etc. They awarded me a £2000 loan, and a £1500 grant.

Throughout the year I create different designs for the events my customers are going to be attending - from nights out with the girls, to races, weddings, raves and holidays. We always have to keep our customer in mind whilst designing new seasons.

I'm always looking at what people are wearing everywhere I go, soaking it up, parks, towns, pubs. I go to London at least once per year, and this year I'm going to Paris and travelling round France by train. My new design ideas come from going to different places, seeing new things, and being out in nature as much as possible.

Photography is my passion too, it's lovely to capture the moment and share what I see that inspires me. And I love living right next to gorgeous Sefton (Sevvy) Park!

8. PRINCES VIEW

Paul Banks, b. 1952

The Banks family story on the Lane starts with the arrival of Paul's grandparents after 1911. His father George and brother Stephen all worked as butchers on the Lane. He recalls playing on the 'plannie' with his friends after watching cowboy films at the Mayfair.

Paul:

I was born in 1952 and lived in 4 Princes View, off Hesketh Street. My grandparents moved to the Lane after 1911, and at least five of their eight children were born here.

My dad, George Banks, was born in 1922 and lived in 13 Princes View until his marriage in 1951. He and my mum Joan then lived in number 4 until 1979. My Aunty Mabel lived at number 8 with my cousins, the Slades, and my Uncle Arthur lived in number 13. In 1979 the street was demolished.

My dad was a butcher, and worked occasionally with me in Duffy's on the Lane. He also worked as a docker. When Jim Duffy retired, my brother Stephen bought the shop and my dad still helped out occasionally.

Bommies

In the picture of Princes View, you can see the scorch marks in the street where we used to have the bonfires for Guy Fawkes Night each year. The 'bommy' used to burn the paint off the front doors unless you kept your front door open.

We used to site the 'bommy' in different places every year, not just in Princes View, but in Hesketh Street and Aigburth View. I can see about six scorch marks on the street!

Princes View, 1969. Paul: 'That's my mum Joan sitting on the steps, talking to 'Aunty Dolly' French. Across the street are Marie Wareing (left) and Audrey Jones (Elaine Geoghegan's mum). Audrey's husband, Cyril, is cleaning his car outside his dad's house. Cyril was the big brother of my pal Tommy.'

The street used to flood in heavy rain. The Victorian drains couldn't cope. I think rainwater and sewage came up into the street. I don't think surface water and sewage were separate in the 1840s. The tin bath that everyone had was used as a boat for playing in too.

The circular area of grass on 'the plannie' was always an island to us lads. We'd put long grass under our snake belts, (remember them?), and roll our kecks up so we had bare legs. We were the native islanders and the other lads were invaders. After seeing cowboy films in the Mayfair, we used to play 'best falling' on the slope into Livingston Drive. Wonderful days!

Mayfair Cinema on Aigburth Road, opened in 1930s, 1969.

9. SEFTON GROVE

The Powell Story:
From Lark Lane to Canada and Frodsham

Tom and Eileen Powell lived on the Lane from the 1930s, and Tom worked as a painter and decorator. Their four children grew up around the Lane from the 1930s to the '60s – Eileen was born in 1937, Fred in 1939, Tom in 1942, and Alan in 1952. In 1955 Eileen married a young Portuguese student and moved to Lisbon. In 1960 she returned to the U.K, so her two children Helena and Jose grew up here, close to their grandparents. In the 1970s Fred, Tom and Alan all decided to emigrate to Canada, where they have remained. Helena now lives in Frodsham with Tony Paxton, and they share a passion for flying. The aerial photos in this volume were taken by them.

Sefton Grove street sign.

Eileen Goncalves, née Powell, b. 1937

Eileen:

I have a thousand happy memories of a wonderful childhood in my beloved Lark Lane. We lived around the corner from Sefton Park in 11 Sefton Grove, so the beautiful Sefton Park was our playground.

Our other playground in wartime and afterwards was the 'debrie' meaning 'debris'. This was a bomb site on Linnet Lane, where beautiful big old houses had once stood. Now it has been rebuilt with pensioners' flats.

Lark Lane was a village; we lived there surrounded by grandparents, aunties and uncles from both sides of the family. It will always be home to me.

Powell family: Eileen with Tom, Alan and Fred.

Tom Powell, b. 1942

'Here's how it happened.'

Our dad Tom Powell Sr. worked as a painter and decorator around the Lane, and was a proud member of the Albert bowling team. He incorporated his business as T.W. Powell & Sons in anticipation of us joining him. But our brother Fred was the only one who became a painter and decorator. And all three of us boys ended up living and working in Canada! Here's how it happened.

In 1962 I was working for a contractor doing house renovations when I found an advertisement recruiting firemen for the Liverpool Fire Brigade. It was very appealing, and looked like an interesting and difficult job. I applied, went through the selection process, and joined the brigade.

The economic situation in Liverpool in the 1970s was bad. Miners' strikes and food shortages, rolling power brownouts, not a good time.

Fred was looking at emigrating to Australia or New Zealand. My wife-to-be, Dorothy Dobson and I, wanted to go to Canada. Fred changed his mind and emigrated to Montreal because he had a friend there, Jim Heptonstall. Jim used to have the sweet shop just down from the Police Station, and had emigrated earlier. Fred rented an apartment and furnished it ready for us, and we emigrated to Montreal in 1974.

Our parents would come out to visit us and they would return to Liverpool brown as berries, with stories about above-ground swimming pools and steaks on a barbecue. I went on to work for the Fire Service in Fredericton, Scarborough and Montreal West, and retired from the Toronto Fire Service as Deputy Fire Chief. Now my daughter Tracey Powell, and my granddaughter Kristy also work in fire prevention. So, since our immigration, our family has contributed greatly to the Canadian Fire Service.

Alan C. Powell, b. 1952

'In 1976, I followed Tom and Fred to Canada.'

I was born in 11 Sefton Grove in 1952. We then moved to 6 Livingston Ave, and my sister Eileen bought 11 Sefton Grove. My brother Tom was ten years older. When I was still at school, I would hear all his stories about working for the Liverpool Fire Brigade. I could tell he loved the job, and the camaraderie.

As I grew up, I helped my dad doing painting and decorating jobs in my spare time. I would paste the paper and as fast as I could paste it, he had the paper on the wall!

At 16 I was fortunate to be selected for a Junior Fireman's 2-year cadet course that included two days per week of college work. I went on to work for the Liverpool Fire Brigade, and then for Merseyside Fire and Rescue Service.

In 1976, I followed Tom and Fred to Canada. I also joined the Canadian Fire Service and retired in 2012 as Fire Captain of the Saint John Fire Department in New Brunswick after 33.5 years. I'm proud to say my son is now a firefighter in my old department!

Alan Powell with a football in Sefton Park.

Helena Paxton, née Goncalves b. 1958

Helena and her brother Jose would go on fishing expeditions to the Fairy Glen. Her grandparents ran a boarding house in Livingston Avenue, where food included rice pudding and 'big pans of proper Scouse'.

Helena:

I was born in January 1958 in Lisbon, Portugal, the home country of my father Luis Goncalves. I grew up predominantly in 11 Sefton Grove. This was originally the home of my grandparents (Nan and Gramps), Tom and Eileen Powell. My mum Eileen grew up there along with her three brothers Freddy, Tommy and Alan.

Eileen first met Luis when he came to Liverpool as a student to study English. They fell in love and married in St. Charles Church on Boxing Day 1955. He whisked her away to Portugal, but Mum was very homesick, so when I was two, they came back to England.

My young parents Eileen and Luis then lived in various places around the Lane, including 25 Hesketh Street and later Livingston Avenue, where my brother was born at home in 1962. They then bought 11 Sefton Grove from my grandparents, who moved in turn to an even larger house in Livingston Avenue.

Fishing in the Fairy Glen

My little brother, Jose Goncalves, was born at home when I was four. I remember hearing his first gusty bawl as he entered the world. As children we would go to Mr. Killey's sweet shop on the Lane to buy long canes with triangular fishing nets attached to one end. Then, with jam jars to put our catch in, we would race off to the Fairy Glen to fish. My brother always caught more 'tiddlers' than I did!

Sugar and Spice

Oh, the Sugar and Spice! A lovely bakery, run by Mr. and Mrs. Stewart. Little Mrs. O'Leary worked there; she was lovely to everyone. She wore a pinny and always smiled. They sold ham and other groceries. There was a big ham slicer behind the counter. You could ask for different thicknesses and they would adjust it accordingly, whizzing off slices onto greaseproof paper. A big glass jar of Oxos sat on the counter top, you could buy just one Oxo if needed. I remember trays of fresh baked bread and an array of cakes. Loved it when Mum took me and my brother shopping in there. I remember Mr. Stewart well, always covered in flour and wore an apron; a smiley man.

Image on left: **View of Lark Lane showing Sefton Grove corner, 1969.**

Shank Soup

I remember Mr. Duffy the butcher as an affable gentleman, always busy, and wore a bloody apron. I used to make patterns in the sawdust on the wooden floor with my feet.

Mum used to ask for bones for the dog, they kept him well fed, and he had lovely white teeth. Mum used to make the most delicious shank soups, with melting potatoes, carrots and onions.

No Tripe for Me!

My dad used to enjoy a plate of tripe, but my brother and I drew the line there!

What has Gramps saved for me today?

When I was a schoolgirl my Nan and Granddad ran a large boarding house in Livingston Avenue. They would take six or seven students from the local technical college, and they had an account with Mr. Duffy. Many a time, on my way back from school I would regularly nip into Nan's before going home, as Gramps would have saved me a knuckle, or a trotter, off a large piece of meat cooking in Nan's big kitchen oven. On occasion, there would be something even better – a pudding such as Angel Delight left over in the fridge and saved for me!

Gramps was still working as a painter and decorator at the time, but he would still peel massive pans of spuds for Nan, whilst watching TV in the back kitchen. One of his sayings to us grandchildren would be 'I've got a bucket of Mars Bars here for you!'

Nana's Role

My Nan kept tropical fish, and was an avid gardener. She always had a really beautiful garden, everyone said she had green fingers. Very organised: she used to sit writing a list, planning the meals ahead for each week: chops, with egg and chips, big pans of proper

Scouse, large joints of lamb, pork shoulder, beef, coupled with vats of the tastiest gravy! I remember roast potatoes right through the week, not just for Sunday!

I also remember large salads, with carved ham, and Nan would cut the tomatoes into stars! There were always plenty of rounds of white bread and real butter, and a large metal teapot, which made 10 plus cuppas. Now I have it, and use it regularly!

Puddings: home-made apple pies, with thick custard, tinned fruit salad with evaporated milk, Angel Delight, and proper sherry trifles with maraschino cherries, or hundreds and thousands. Home-made rice pudding, with a thick skin on top, which we kids would fight over. Nan and Gramps had also ran a successful fruit and veg shop in the '60s, and later a newsagents on 69 Lark Lane!

In Sight of the Hale Lighthouse

Now I live in Frodsham. From my window I can see Liverpool Cathedral and the Hale Lighthouse, where my grandparents had such fun with their friends in their courting days in the '30s.

Hale Lighthouse, 2020.

The White Family, Robert (Bob) Stephen White, b. 1953

Bob grew up across the street from the Police Station, so the pool table in the coppers' recreation room was a tempting destination for a bold lad. Later he worked as a delivery boy (on a bike) for Platt's the butchers.

Robert:

I was born on June 10, 1953 in 3 Sefton Grove. I had a younger brother, Gordon, and a sister, Beryl. You can read her story below about our great-grandmother Frances.

My father, Frederick White, came from Whittlesey, near Peterborough. He met my future mum Dorothy Halcrow, who had grown up in Lucerne Street, when she was working down there as a land army girl. He moved up to Liverpool and they got married in Christ Church in Linnet Lane.

My mum's family, my grandparents Josie and Ralph Halcrow, lived in 28 Lucerne Street, and my great-grandmother Frances McPherson Batten (known as Nin to us) lived across the road at number 35.

Bells for Servants

When Dad was decorating the top bedroom, he noticed a crack in the plaster. Behind the plaster we found some thin metal wires. We traced these down to the cellar, where they went behind some wooden paneling. We took the paneling off and found some tags marked Master Bedroom, Back Bedroom, and Dining Room. They had once contained bells for the gentry of the house to call the servants from downstairs, it's a pity we did not take a picture of them, as they are probably gone now!

Keeping Warm

The cellar had a big open range fire with a side oven for cooking. When a fire was lit, you could feel the heat in the chimney breasts in the bedrooms.

Who Lived Where

Margaret Foy lived in number 1, the Whites were at number 3, and Mr. and Mrs. Burke in number 5. The O'Sullivans lived at number 7, number 9 lived a Mrs. Skinner and the Morgans, number 11 lived the Powell family and in number 13 lived the Bentley family.

The other side of the Grove was Lark Lane Police Station, with living accommodation. The Spences lived there, as Mr. John Spence was a policeman.

The police station had its own canteen and cooks for the policemen on duty. My mum would often tap on the canteen window to borrow a pint of milk at night, and often a cook would knock on our door to borrow a cup of sugar for the "night bobbies".

Quick, the Coppers are Coming!

The police station had a recreation room with a full-size pool table and table tennis. We would often sneak in there for a quick game of pool, but the real fun was getting out of there without getting a boot up the backside when the coppers came in. Most of our time was spent in Sefton Park and Otterspool. Times were good.

First Jobs

When I was old enough, I got a paper round with Mr. Wilkinson. My round was Sefton Park. The big houses around the Park were amazing, so big and ornate. Later I worked as a delivery boy for Platt's the butchers. We used Billy the Fish's bike ['Billy the Fish' was their nickname for Mr. Billy Carmichael at Glendinning's], as Platt's were too tight to buy their own!

Beryl Byrne, née White b. 1963

Beryl is a keeper of many memories of her great-grandmother Frances Batten. Here are two.

Stories of My Great-Grandmother

I was born Beryl White in 1963 at 3 Sefton Grove. I had two older brothers, Bob and Gordon. My mother, Dorothy White, née Halcrow, is now 89.

My great–grandmother Frances Batten (whom we called Nin), often visited us in Sefton Grove and lived at 35 Lucerne Street. She lived until I was thirteen. My cousin Joan has written about her. Here is an early story about her when she was a young widow.

Frances Matilda Rowland was born on 11 June 1883 at 18 Harding Street, West Derby. Her mother Elizabeth Ann worked as a laundress, and signed with her 'mark' on the birth certificate. Frances married Robert Macpherson and had three children: Elizabeth, born in 1905, Josephine, in 1906 (Josie, my grandmother), and Robert Jr., born in 1908. In 1910 Robert Sr. died, so at the age of 27 Frances became a widow responsible for providing for three young children.

Frances Matilda Rowland as a young woman.

At that time Frances was working as a washerwoman in one of the big houses for a Mr. Kipling, who was employed in the metal industry. When she had finished her day's washing, she would take the slither of soap she had used that day back home, along with crusts of bread that the cook gave her.

A neighbour, who called into her home for a chat, later reported her for taking the soap! When Frances went into work the next day, the cook told her she had to go to Mr. Kipling.

Frances was very upset, fearing she would lose her job. Mr. Kipling asked her about the soap. She explained it was only the slither of soap she took. Mr. Kipling, after hearing of her situation as a widow with three children to support, said "From now on, please take a whole bar of soap a week. And every day, you can take a loaf of bread and any leftovers you want."

So, the good neighbour did her a favour! Frances left her soap on show for all to see!

In 1915 she married Arthur Clement Batten and had three more children: Arthur in 1915, Ernest in 1918, and William (Billy), in 1922. They all lived at 45 Bickerton Street. During WW2, her two youngest sons died on active service, Billy in 1942 in the loss of the Avenger, and Ernie in 1943 when the Empress of Canada was torpedoed.

Bomb in Siddeley Street

When the bomb dropped on Siddeley Street during the Blitz, the 'All Clear' had already been sounded. My great-nan Frances was in her kitchen in Lucerne Street making tea when there was an explosion. Her door had blown off, and there was a mangle up her hallway. A neighbour in Livingston Drive reported something on a chimney in Lucerne Street. It was a tablecloth. Underneath was a man's body.

10. SIDDELEY STREET

Lindsey Rimmer, née Walsh, b. 1949

Lindsey has lived in this area all her life and attended St. Charles School and Sunday parades at St. Clare's Church. She grew up at a time when you went everywhere by bus, and the Waiting Room was in constant use.

Lindsey:

I was born in 1949 in 21 Siddeley Street, the fourth of five siblings. When my mum left County Wicklow and moved to Liverpool in 1937, she first lived at the top of Lark Lane. She was a qualified nurse.

I went to St. Charles, starting at South Grange in 1954. We left Lark Lane in 1964, but moved only a short distance to Aigburth Road, opposite the army barracks. After I got married, our family home was in Langham Avenue.

I still wander up the Lane frequently.

The Waiting Room

The Waiting Room was quite big (well it was to me). It was half-moon shape, and was at the end of the Lane, from Aigburth Road, around to Livingston Drive. It was quite tall and had a brown wooden bench across the back wall. I guess you could seat maybe 15-20 people. There were two glass doors in the middle, with high windows all around. There were two bus stops for buses 20, 25 and 82, 87, 500 and Crossville H1.

The 60 going to Bootle terminus stopped opposite the Gaumont in Dingle Lane, then turned onto Parkfield Rd from Aigburth Road at Lark Lane. I can't remember if the 500 Limited stop was running before the road improvement. I would use the 60 to go to Guides off Gainsborough Rd.

There were a few of us who would be always late for Sunday parade at St Clare's Church, as the buses were few and far between on a Sunday.

I would also use the 82c to get to either Garston baths or to Speke Hall.

If you got the H1, it would go past the pea picking farms outside Hale village.

Right behind the waiting room were the smelliest toilets you could ever imagine. You walked down into them. They were awful! (At the Dingle bus sheds there were toilets, big green doors, and they were well kept.)

On the Livingston Drive side there were two red phone boxes, the 60 bus would park up there. It was where you could get 1/- for the meter.

The Waiting Room was removed when the dual carriageway was built.

Charlie Jolley with his daughters Ada (mother of Lynne Bywater) and Dorothy, known as Marge.

Lynne Bywater, b. 1950

In the 1950s, when the police houses were under construction in the street, Lynne and her friends would climb in as soon as the builders packed up their tools and left for the day. One more playground!

Lynne:

I was born in 1950 and lived at 17 Siddeley Street. I have very fond memories of playing in the Lane with Lindsey and Alison Walsh. Skipping with the rope tied to the lamp post. We played in the police houses when they were being built. After the builders left for the day, we would go exploring. 'No Health and Safety then!'

The lady next door to us, Mrs. Thomas, used to sharpen her knife on the step and make a line so that you didn't walk on her step. She used to chase us away from her door. Her son Frank would yodel as he went down the yard.

My great-granddad Henry Jolley was a slater and plasterer. From what I've been told, he did the grapes frieze in the Albert. My granddad, Charlie, was a blacksmith and farrier.

My mum, Ada Jolley, was born in the house. During the war she went to London and served as a messenger in the Air Ministry. Her first husband was in the bomb disposal unit. A bomb he was defusing exploded. He lived for 7 more years. Mum's sister Aunty Marg, lived here during the war. She worked on Spitfires.

Their brother Walter took part in the Liberation of Belsen. Charlie was in Wingate's forgotten army in Burma. My uncle Geoff was present in the Battle of the Atlantic. Where would we be now if not for all those who served!

Marg Hibbert, née Kelly b. 1952

Marg's father was a policeman with the nickname of Crunchie and she grew up in one of the three new police houses. Her best friend Mary Willingham lived in Lucerne Street, and she met her future husband Reg Hibbert at the Albert. In 2021 they celebrate their 49th wedding anniversary.

Marg:

I was born in 1952, and grew up in Siddeley Street in one of the three police houses built on the bombed site. Dad worked in Lark Lane Police Station. He was known to his mates as Crunchie, because that was how he liked his toast!

We lived next door to the Russells. My best friend as we grew up was Mary Willingham from Lucerne St. She went to work in the Albert to get some money for our holidays. That's when I met Reg Hibbert. Dick and Edie Royal ran it then.

We were married in 1972 and are still together. Mary met and married Stuart Russell and they are still together. And we are still all friends!

Overleaf: 'Kites above Otterspool Promenade.' Alex Corina, 2020.

'In life we cannot avoid change, we cannot avoid loss. Freedom and happiness are found in the flexibility and ease with which we move through change.'

Jack Kornfield, *Buddha's Little Instruction Book*, Bantam, nd. p.78

IV | GLOBAL VILLAGE: THE LANE IN 2020

IV | THE LANE IN 2020

During the Pandemic

Here are Facebook entries from Lark Lane residents and former residents following the first two months of the global lockdown. They are writing from the Canary Islands, Lark Lane, Ottawa, Canada, and Vallejo, California, recording their daily lives in a new and dangerous environment.

Marianne Ruscoe - Las Palmas de Gran Canaria, Canary Islands

Monday, March 16

Schools closed Thursday. We've been in total isolation since Saturday! Only supermarkets, pharmacy and emergency services open. Police are patrolling.

Army down south of the island to prevent tourists from leaving hotels and going to the beach. Spot fine €100 up to €6000 if they're not satisfied with your reason for being outside! Oh, you can walk your dog though, that's the only exception! You can't nip around to your friends or family for a coffee or company.

A couple over the road have relatives with children staying, so they can all support each other through this time! Don't think tourists are coming to the island any more, just flying people back home! The warehouses are still functioning and I think we are still receiving freight.

We're a small island with only two hospitals. We've had one death and numbers are climbing with the infection. I'm not going anywhere.

I run the shop like something out of Benny Hill. Everyone moves out of each other's way. One-meter rule! It's a strange feeling, like limbo, not knowing what the outcome is going to be!

Keep safe, everyone. Keep washing your hands and don't touch your face.

I'm getting used to it now. At first, not touching your face is like someone saying to you 'Don't look at the telly!' Ha! X

Maranto's, 57-63 Lark Lane

The 'Swiss cottage' style building on the Lane started life as the Christ Church Institute run by the Christ Church congregation on Linnet Lane, and opened in 1884. It was sold in the 1960s. For the last 37 years, Steve and Ruth Maranto have run it, and the adjoining building, as a family-owned and operated Italian-American restaurant.

March 21

Maranto's closed, in accordance with the government directive. On their website they wrote:

Rest assured, we will be back, as soon as we possibly can. Maranto's has been, and forever will be, a place for families of all sorts, from our customers...to our loyal staff, many of whom have been with us for years and make us who we are.

Sue O'Hagan remembers when they first opened in 1983:

I worked in Barry Hayden Hairdressers at the time. When I moved to work in McGuffie's Chemist, we used to pop to Maranto's for lunch. Over the years, many a happy night's been spent there, including my fiftieth birthday party.

Alex Corina, visual artist in residence, The Amorous Cat Gallery, 47 Lark Lane

Working on the Lane

I was born in Bradford and started off by studying printmaking at the Regional College of Art. I moved to Liverpool 35 years ago. From 1979–2003, however, I was deeply involved in public health issues, and I did not become a full-time artist until 2004. I'm best known for my Mona Lennon, produced for Liverpool's Capital of Culture in 2008.

The recent history of 33 Lark Lane from 2002 until now, is part of the rich tapestry that is Lark Lane. First was Frances Conway-Seymour with the Lark Lane Atelier, then I ran Lark Lane Art Works in the Atelier until 2018. For the past two years, Sally Ayres has been running number 33 as Freida Mo's. In November 2019, Jan

Lark Lane Atelier.

and Ron Sears opened The Amorous Cat Gallery at 47 Lark Lane. I am currently artist in residence and exhibit my work there, along with six other artists. I also have work in Keith's wine bar (my office).

A year or so ago, I started a transcription of 'The Card Players' after Cezanne, basing my version on Keith's Wine Bar. I started with a few drawings. The actors are Mario, Deni, Carl and Russell.

Four pencil drawings by Alex Corina. Mario *(top left)*, Deni *(top right)*, Carl *(bottom left)* and Russell *(bottom right)*.

I also made many drawings of musicians playing at Keith's.

Three musicians at Keith's. Buster on flute *(top left)*, Hugo on bass *(top right)*, and Tony on trumpet.

Frances Conway-Seymour

Frances was a bohemian 'old school' artist who landed in Liverpool in 2003, the year of Liverpool's successful bid to become European Capital of Culture 2008. She moved from Bristol and established the Lark Lane Atelier at number 33. Perfect timing! Frances would sit at a desk in the gallery waiting for someone to come in to look at the art and start talking. She loved encouraging other artists, and she loved a good argument about art!

Frances Conway-Seymour.

Frances was also a campaigner. I will never forget her painting banners with locals in the gallery, and going out in the dead of night flyer posting. They were protesting against the sell-off of a bit of Sefton Park for housing.

In her previous life in Bristol, she was married to the writer and environmentalist John Seymour, commonly known as 'The Father of Self-Sufficiency.' John lived a varied and fascinating life: writer, broadcaster, agrarian, smallholder and activist. A rebel against consumerism, industrialisation, genetically modified organisms, cities, motor cars. And an advocate for: self-reliance, personal responsibility, self-sufficiency, conviviality (food, drink, dancing and singing), gardening, caring for the Earth and for the soil.

Frances was a legend, and the Lane loved her. She died in 2010. Her daughter Helen studied music at LIPA and is a talented musician still living locally.

Walking from Garston to the Lane
March 26, 7:25am

Early start on the prom. I see Prince Charles tested positive for coronavirus, as have politicians, an assortment of footballers and famous folks. Yet the government can't/won't make available tests to NHS staff at the sharp end, whom they say they value so much! It's about 3.5 to 4 miles from Garston to the Garden Festival site, and 10 minutes from Lark Lane when you can cut through. But gates don't open till 8.30am, so I head back. Pre-pandemic, I'd set off later and head to Lark Lane and round the Park. You can walk almost all the way to the Albert Dock on the prom except for a short detour at the Brunswick Dock, then from the Marina through to the Three Graces.

Alex Corina, Otterspool Promenade, looking towards Runcorn.

Sally Ayres - Freida Mo's Tea Room, Bakery and Vintage Shop

Over the past two years, 33 Lark Lane has become a social hub, realising the dream of its enterprising and community-minded owner Sally Ayres. In her early years Sally ran a non-profit dance and theatre school near Brighton. After moving to Liverpool in 2007, she studied entertainment management. She went on to organise and run vintage auctions, selling online and at festivals, including Glastonbury. Freida Mo's offers a friendly tea shop with a focus on conversation, as well as a way of expressing her love of vintage fashion and her passion for recycling.

Sally Ayres:

Lark Lane is a really interesting place to get used to. It has its own politics. There is a solid community around here, but no one has really taken charge of it. Making people feel like they're part of a family is the most important part of this shop to me. In a city it can feel so empty - I felt like it was my duty to bring people together. And it still is!

April 1

Today I come with sad news - last night my privacy and my life were destroyed! Someone broke into Freida Mo's! Things were taken of value, but more to the point I feel violated. At times like this, with no money coming in and no one to fix the door because everyone is out of work, I'm now completely vulnerable. I need help ... in any form ... so please send it, even if it's loving thoughts.

The community rallied instantly. In two days, enough funds were donated to enable repairs to be carried out. Sally got straight back into her kitchen and started baking for Easter deliveries.

Lynn Brown Lawrenson - Ottawa, Canada

April 1

All are in isolation here apart from going for essentials. Sad I can't book my ticket for July but hopefully can go later in the year.

I spend my time cleaning, washing, watching the news on CTV, CNN and anything else that comes on, and talking on the phone. I call my Aunty Ada in Liverpool every few days to make sure she is OK. She still lives on the Lane, and is 92.

Caroline Oates - Studio off Bold Street, Liverpool

April 4

Today I decided to go back to my studio, as the government guidelines are only go to work if you cannot work from home. I work alone, as most of you know, so social distancing is not an issue!

Good job I did go back in, as I was called upon to help with NHS protective clothing. I know it's only a small thing, but if I hadn't gone to my studio then I would not have been able to help.

Elastic was needed to make the strap on the plastic protector for key workers. I was able to throw the elastic out of the window, so no contact and then a few hours later 25 masks have been made for staff at the Royal Hospital! I feel so happy that I have been of some use in the fight against this virus. Every small gesture, no matter how small, really does make a big difference.

Maranto's. KF

Kay Flavell - Vallejo, California

March 31

My evening walk tonight takes me along an historic South Vallejo shoreline that was once busy with a flourmill and sailing ships. On his honeymoon in May 1880, the Scottish author Robert Louis Stevenson and his bride Fanny spent a night in a workman's hotel here, en route to their honeymoon in Calistoga and an abandoned miner's cottage. They were kept awake by the croaking of frogs from the marshes. Stevenson recorded the waterfront scene:

> There was a tall building beside the pier, labeled the STARR FLOUR MILLS; and sea-going, full-rigged ships lay close along shore, waiting for their cargo. Soon these would be plunging round the Horn, soon the flour from the STARR FLOUR MILLS would be landed on the wharfs of Liverpool. For that, too, is one of England's outposts; thither, to this gaunt mill, across the Atlantic and Pacific deeps and round about the icy Horn, this crowd of great, three-masted, deep-sea ships come, bringing nothing, and return with bread.

From Vallejo I head for Raley's grocery supermarket in Benicia, our neighbouring historic town. It lies on the shores of the mighty Sacramento River, as it finds its way to the ocean via Carquinez Strait. Before the bridges, this stretch was called Silvergate.

Port of loading: Starr Mills in South Vallejo.

Silvergate. Looking from Benicia towards the Carquinez Bridge, San Pablo Bay, and the Golden Gate opening onto the Pacific Ocean.

Port of arrival: Liverpool docks. Historic image showing St. Nicholas Church.

I walk at dusk down First Street to the Union Hotel and back. Out come Venus and the Moon. Calm dark night. Ghostly buildings date back to Gold Rush days, when a ferry across to Benicia enabled you to continue your trek up to the goldfields, (and later the silver mines), of Sacramento and Nevada.

April 12

I've just watched the moving address of Queen Elizabeth II and I would like to repeat her lovely greeting 'Happy Easter to people of all faiths and all nations.'

I have been fortunate to be a citizen of three nations - New Zealand, the UK and the USA. Deep bonds link me with friends and family in all three. My faith as a story collector is expressed in the words of Namaste - 'I honour the place in you of light, of peace and of truth.'

I light this candle for you, people from around Lark Lane, those living in Liverpool and those who are now all around the world. How and where are you spending these days, celebrating light and life in a time of great danger?

> *When you walk through a storm*
> *Hold your head up high*
> *And don't be afraid of the dark.*
> *At the end of the storm*
> *Is a golden sky*
> *And the sweet silver song of the lark.*

'You'll never walk alone,' from *Carousel*, 1945.
Gerry and the Pacemakers, 1963.

Easter Candle.

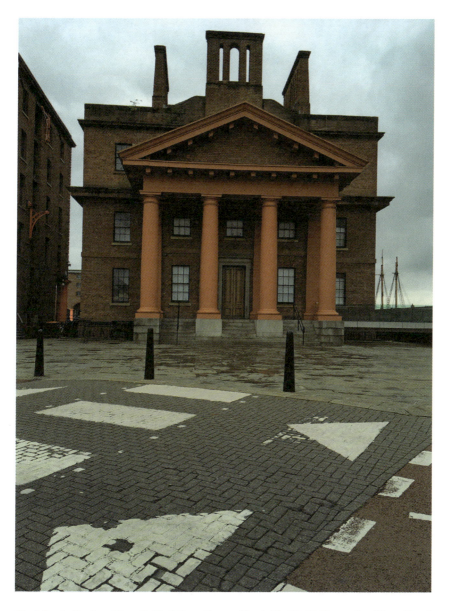

Dr. Martin Luther King, Jr. Building, former Dock Traffic Office at the Albert Dock. A ten-year Waterfront Transformation Project was launched by Museums Liverpool in March 2021.

Overleaf: Albert Dock in 2019.

V | POSTSCRIPT: REIMAGINING LIVERPOOL

V REIMAGINING LIVERPOOL

You can change your life down to your last breath.
Bertolt Brecht. 'Everything Changes'

A city's built form changes over time, as does the social life of those who live there. New uses are found for old houses, old clothes and old books. Trash becomes treasure.

The stories we tell ourselves about who we are, where we have come from, and where we are going also change. Consider the ways in which two traditional story patterns – romance and adventure – have been put to new uses to show changing gender roles over the past century.

1900 fictional models: A traditional romance story pattern divided women's ideal lives into three stages: childhood; a period of romance; and an uneventful aftermath of 'living happily ever after' with a single partner. Heterosexuality was the norm. Single women were seen as 'old maids', objects of pity and sometimes scorn. If they featured in adventure stories, as in *True Stories of Girl Heroines*, the adventures were seen only as episodes leading towards romantic endings. Single men were presented as the heroes of adventure narratives, as in ancient epics, but often these ended by blending with a traditional heterosexual romance narrative. Ulysses came home to Penelope.

1900 social norms: When women entered higher education and started leading working professional lives from the 1880s on, they had to start shaping new life stories that broke with the Victorian division of 'women at home' and 'men at work'. Working-class women had never fitted the norm, as Mrs. Margaret McLean points out:

'We always had to work.' Male gender norms were equally limiting. Until the mid-20th century, male homosexuality was regarded as a crime in the UK. Bisexuality and same-sex partnerships between women were socially invisible and kept secret.

Fast forward through many waves of feminism and gay liberation to the 2020 world of LBGTQ diversity! Young people growing up today know they are the authors of their own life stories. We tell them that the limits of the possible are defined only by their imagination.

When I started interviewing people on Lark Lane forty years ago, I was often met with "My story isn't interesting, because I'm just an ordinary person." I kept listening, because I wanted to capture the special character of that life. Sixteen years spent teaching in four countries - in Christchurch, New Zealand; Saarbrücken, Germany; a term in a secondary modern school in Orpington, South London; a decade at the University of London and a year in Princeton, New Jersey - had taught me that every one of us is a dreamer. I waited for the moments when the speaker revealed how their life had brought fulfillment or disappointment of their dream. No life is 'ordinary'. We are all in process.

As members of each new city generation develop their own sense of individual and collective identity by finding their way through the social worlds of family, school, popular culture and work, the city street is a key point of intersection. Right from the start, it's also the area of turf disputes. "Go play up your own end!" was the angry shout that many Lark Lane children heard all too often from their elders if they moved their play area a few houses further up or down their own street. My young friends, the world is not so small. Back off now, but keep exploring!

As an educator, I believe my most important task is to give everyone an expanded sense of possible lives for themselves and those around them. Learn to see and walk around the walls that others seek to put up around you!

Here is an anecdote. In 1972, I made my first visit to Liverpool. I was a wife, mother of a six-month-old child, and held a tenured lecturing job in London. Our home was in Islington, a 15-minute bus ride from my job. My husband, a fellow academic in London, had just been offered a job by Liverpool University. I was stunned when a senior professor in my field scorned my wish to continue my current academic research. He made two unforgettable comments: 'Of course you'll give up your job in London. Wives always follow husbands!' Next, 'There are only two places to live in Liverpool, A or B.' Such narrow thinking! Male chauvinism on full display! I hung onto my job in London and chose commuting. I received severe criticism from some faculty wives for breaking a social norm. But 'Keep going, Kay, you give us hope,' said another wife, a member of a women's group who were engaged in a similar fight to reshape women's lives and women's stories in the interests of gender equality and social justice.

Since 1981 the process of reimagining Liverpool as a river city has focused on two initiatives: a short-lived 1984 Garden Festival project adjoining the Otterspool Promenade in what is now known as the Riverside parliamentary constituency, and an ongoing project to reimagine the abandoned warehouses and mud-filled wasteland of the historic Albert Dock as a world-class tourist destination lined with museums, hotels and restaurants, as well as a well-lit waterfront promenade.

Straight after the Toxteth riots of 1981, then Secretary of State for the Environment, Sir Michael Heseltine and his team, visited Liverpool and set up a Merseyside Task Force to work for revitalisation. Planning began for an International Garden Festival on 230 acres of landfill (created from excavations for the Mersey Tunnel), between Jericho Lane and the old Herculaneum Dock. The Festival was opened by Queen Elizabeth II in May 1984 and brought 3.4 million visitors to the site over the next five months. After it closed, the site was neglected. Some of the land has since been developed for housing and more is planned by its owners, Liverpool City Council, though there are severe pollution issues still to be addressed.

Downtown, the dream of Liverpool as a tourist destination began to take shape with the transformation of Jesse Hartley's impressive Albert Dock, once again filled with water, into a cultural hub. The Merseyside Maritime Museum opened in 1984, and Tate Liverpool opened in 1988. A new Museum of Liverpool opened on the waterfront in 2011. That process has continued with the opening of the International Slavery Museum, and the Beatles Museum.

Liverpool's city centre has remained a walkable city. A 20-minute walk from the waterfront brings you past the 1717 Bluecoat building in School Lane and up the hill to the stunning 19th century cluster of libraries, museums and galleries stretching from St. George's Hall along William Brown Street. This is Liverpool's equivalent of the Bloomsbury district in London, the Georgian squares surrounding the British Museum.

But to see the realised vision of a 19th century synthesis of landscape and cityscape, you must make your way out to Sefton Park via a 40-minute walk or by train, bus or car. Just as New York's Central Park and Brooklyn's Prospect Park demonstrate the continuing viability of the democratic social vision and architectural brilliance of Frederick Law Olmsted and Calvert Vaux, so Sefton Park's green world of trees, shrubs, lake and winding paths, as imagined in the late 1860s by Lewis Hornblower and Edouard André, remains a treasured place for everyone to feel at home in every season.

Corner of Sefton Park. KF

Swans on the Lake.

Journey from Silvergate, October 2019

From shining Silvergate
and towers of San Francisco
I cross by silver bird
to a quiet London garden
near Primrose Hill.
Then north by train to Liverpool
and a small white room
on Seymour Street.

Grey mornings
woken by seagulls.
High above the Mersey
two copper cormorants
keep watch:
Bella gazes seaward,
Bertie watches crowds
on Paradise Street.

New boots on cobblestones.
This week I walk the Mersey shore.
In Albert Dock
old ships are anchored
beside a carousel.
Central Library is overflowing
with young voices.
City of students, city of ghosts.

KF October 2019

List of Telephone Subscribers in Lark Lane Exchange from NTCo Directory of 1899.

From a handwritten list prepared by Stanley Roberts of Eastham on 1 March 1982.

38	Aigburth Steam Laundry	Aigburth Road
212	Anderson, Frederick J.	32 Linnet Lane
52	Anderson, J. Edward	11 Alexandra Drive
235	Appleby, Fred	1 Marmion Road
87	Ashby, Charles	55 Parkfield Road
84	Bath, James Parker, Coach Proprietor	7 Aigburth Vale
156	Batty, R. & Sons, Cow Keepers & Farmers	Batty's Dairy, Aigburth Road
204	Beaty, Richard	Kirklinton, Aigburth Drive
125	Beaumont, Lewis, G., Merchant	12 Livingston Drive
99	Beavan, W.F.	Deepdene, Sandringham Drive
214	Beer, A.D., Cotton Merchant	17 Linnet Lane
142	Belcher, Edmund C.	9 Normanton Avenue
79	Beloe, Chas, H.	11 Livingston Drive
104	Bingham, D.A.	31 Alexandra Drive
193	Bissett, Mrs. Fanny, Registry Office	72 Lark Lane
121	Blundell, Fred B., Meat Purveyor	28 Aigburth Road
88	Blyth, John	Coiro, Aigburth Road
172	Booth, Chas.	Otterspool Bank, St Michael's
249	Bowen, William, Outfitter	19 Fulwood Park
144	Bowring, Chas W.	Chislehurst, Aigburth Drive
110	Brodie, John A.	Calder Lodge, 28 Ullet Road
31	Brogden, Mrs.	7 Fulwood Park
94	Brookfield, M. A., Grocers, Wines, Spirits	Post Office, Aigburth
250	Brookfield, M. A., Grocer, Provision Dealer	1A Fulwood Road
225	Browne, H. Nedeham	3 Ivanhoe Road
240	Burke, Thomas, Poulterer & Fruiterer	Aigburth Road
145	Burrows, H.F.	26 Marmion Road
136	Bury, Mrs	Hyndburn, Aigburth Road
203	Bushby, Miss	22 Linnet Lane
192	Bussweiler, Alfred	15 Linnet Lane
215	Byrom, Edward, Pork Butcher	134 Aigburth Road
77	Cadman, C.W.	18 Linnet Lane
109	Cahill, Mrs., Cook & Confectioner	76 Lark Lane
60	Cain, Alfred, D., Brewer	Barn Hey, Aigburth Road
106	Cain, Herbert	9 Sandringham Drive
163	Cain, W.E.	15 Ivanhoe Road, Sefton Park
135	Cain's Branch, Albert Hotel	68 Lark Lane, Sefton Park
114	Camenisch, J.	8 Aigburth Drive

101	Cameron, Nelson	Fassifern, Aigburth Vale
18	Cappel, Louis (Gruning & Co)	5 Ullet Road
252	Carey, Eustace, Alkali Manufacturer	20 Alexandra Drive
38	Carrie, G.G., The Hamlet Supply Stores	124 Aigburth Road
35	Carruthers, J., Fish Poultry & Game	12 Lark Lane
251	Chilton, Thomas, Merchant	2 Aigburth Drive
10	Clark, W. C.	Orleans House, Aigburth Drive
9	Clarkson, Wm.	The Friars, St Michael's Hamlet
231	Clayton, John H.	Adlington, Livingston Drive
115	Clegg's Stores, Groceries & Provisions	64 Lark Lane
78	Clough, Alfred, Works Manager	74 Lark Lane, Sefton Park
59	Cohan, E. A.	16 Linnet Lane
152	Cohen, L. S.	The Priory, St Michael's
184	Cole, G. H.	11 Ivanhoe Road
123	Corkhill, John, Builder & Contractor	Errol Street, Toxteth Park
80	Cornelius, R.	2 Livingston Drive
229	Cottrell & Beszant, Safety Boiler Makers	11 Aigburth Vale
37	Crosfield, W.	Annesley, Woodlands Road
32	Cross, Frank, R.	15 Fulwood Park
54	Dart, Richard	Terceira, Aigburth Drive
167	Davies, D. L., Furnishings, Ironmonger	60 Lark Lane
122	Davies, John R., Butcher	18 Lark Lane
241	Davis, J. H. (Davis Ltd)	5 Eastfield Drive, Sefton Park
71	Davison, W. H.	Derwent House, Aigburth Drive
22	Dawson, Ralph, M.	23 Fulwood Park, Aigburth
179	Deacon, Henry Wade	8 Ullet Road
226	Deakin, J. Buckley	14 Ullet Road
166	Decker, Hermann, Merchant	4 Parkfield Road, Princes Park
4	Doughty, Alex	Ledard, Sefton Park
238	Eckes, John B.	22 Alexandra Drive
191	Edgar, S. Edgar, General Merchant	22 Southwood Road, St Michael's
91	Edmonson, E.	The Woodlands, Aigburth
29	Edwards, T. H.	6 Beech Lawn, Elmswood Road
178	Eills, Burton, W.	East Bank, Sefton Park
230	Elley, M. J.	St Michael's Mount, Southwood Rd
53	Ellis & Co.	88 Lark Lane
69	Fachiri, Cleopatra N.	Livingston Drive
182	Fairrie, A. J.	63 Parkfield Road
189	Fernie, Henry	17 Alexandra Drive
244	Fischer, John Jacob, Merchant	12 Sandringham Drive
147	Fletcher, A. Piggott	Keran Ila, Sefton Park
196	Forster, J. G.	Southlands, Aigburth Road
186	Foulkes, Pedro, Merchant	Boa Vista, Livingston Drive
11	Fowler, Mrs William	1 Alexandra Drive
159	Gamble, J. A., Fruiterer	136 Aigburth Road
139	Gaskell, T. F., Solicitor	61 Parkfield Road
258	Gibbons, Herbert H., (Gibbons & Arkle)	9 Parkfield Road
128	Gibson, Ernest, Barrister-at-Law	1 East Albert Road
56	Gibson, Thomas, Gentleman	Granton, Aigburth Drive

34	Gladstone, Robert	24 Alexandra Drive, Ullet Road
42	Glendinning, J. & H., Fishmongers & Poulterers	91 Lark Lane
157	Gow, Wm.	8 Livingston Drive North
21	Graham, John, Sugar Refiner	Aigburth Drive
188	Grainger, David, Shipowner	Culmore, Princes Park
222	Hacking, Edward, Cotton Broker	1 Windermere Terrace
47	Hakes, James, Surgeon	Latrigg, Aigburth Road
236	Hammond, H. H., Merchant	Valparaiso Ho, Aigburth Drive
143	Handley, William, Grocer, Provision Dealer	154 Aigburth Road
72	Harrison, T. F., Merchant	8 Linnet Lane, Sefton Park
245	Hawley & Son, Chemists	Fulwood Pharmacy, Aigburth Road
153	Haythorne, Thos., Physician & Surgeon	Hazelmere, Aigburth Road
7	Henderson, Francis	4 Alexandra Drive
103	Hewitt, George H.	Woodlands Road, Aigburth
12	Heyworth, G. B	Holm Lea, Aigburth Drive
64	Holt, George	8 Fulwood Park
213	Hornby, E. C.	Kingsley, Ashfield Road
51	Hough, Samuel	Arequipa, Aigburth Road
199	Hughes, Thomas, JP	Springwood, Linnet Lane
85	Humby, Herbert D., Fruiterer & Florist	156 Aigburth Road
162	Huxley's Stores, Provision Merchants	142 Aigburth Road
175	Inglis, A. G., Solicitor	28 Marmion Road
143	Irvine, Thos.	Glenhuntley, Aigburth Road
163	Isaacson, John, Bank Manager	Wantley, Parkfield Road
218	Jackson, A. M., General Produce Broker	23 Marmion Road
248	Jago, A. E.	15 Parkfield Road
246	Japp, John	9 Alexandra Drive
187	Jennings, Joseph, Baker, Flour dealer	Aigburth Road
75	Joanides, S.	10 Livingston Drive
194	Jones, H. Lee J.	10 Bertram Road
185	Jones, James, Chemist	112 Aigburth Road
195	Key, M. E., Boot, Shoe Dealer	152 Aigburth Road
137	Kidman, J, Marine Insurance Secretary	8 Livingston Drive North
197	Kilgour, L. J.	65 Parkfield Road
150	Kirkland, Baker to Queen	6 Fulwood Park
198	Kramrisch, S. [Camenisch], Merchant	19 Linnet Lane
228	Lambert, Mrs, Servants Agency	10 Aigburth Vale
129	Langhorn, Jackson, Fruiterer & Greengrocers	113 Lark Lane
258	Larrinaga, Theodoro de	23 Alexandra Drive
208	Lawrence, Edward	The Grange, St Michael's
216	Lee, J. & Son, Stationers & Printers	150 Aigburth Road
24	Lee, Mary Buchanan, Physician & Surgeon	39 Ivanhoe Road, Sefton Park
49	Levy, Elliott	Lismore, Sefton Park
126	Lewis, D. L.	Holme Lea, Aigburth Drive
45	Lewis, Samuel, Meat Purveyor	103 Lark Lane
44	Liverpool Corporation Offices	Lark Lane, Toxteth Park
2	Lockett, R. R.	26 Alexandra Drive
107	Long, Simpson & Fowler, Plumbers, Painters & Dec's	117 Lark Lane
140	Luthy, Hans	3 Hargreaves Road

219	McDougall, Jr Edlington, Physician & Surgeon	South Grange, Aigburth Road
155	MacDuff, R.	5 Fulwood Park
83	Macfie, Rodie	Windermere House, Princes Park
259	Magnus, Arthur	Florida, Aigburth Drive
247	Martin, Dr. J. Graham, Physician & Surgeon	83 Aigburth Road
27	Melladew, Mrs E.	Lynewood, Aigburth Drive
169	Miller, J. J.	13 Alexandra Drive
157	Moffat, Wm., Cotton Broker	Kenmore, Aigburth Drive
13	Monro-Lowe, G. H., Surgeon	99 Aigburth Road
149	Moore, W. F.	1 Fulwood Park
66	Morris, John	33 Parkfield Road
15	Moss, Wm. M.	St Modwens, Aigburth Drive
43	Murdoch, William Hughes, MD	2 Southwood Road, St Michael's
111	Nelson, Phillip, MB, Surgeon	2 Aigburth Vale
205	Nevanas, Thomas	4 Southwood Road, St Michael's
98	Nicholsons, G	Parkside, Ullet Road
30	Norman, Mrs. William	13 Hargreaves Road
46	Norris, Robert, Solicitor	7 Ullet Road
116	Nurses Home	2 Livingston Avenue, Sefton Park
28	Oliver, John B., MD	59 Parkfield Road
254	Page, J. B.	20 Roxburgh Avenue
134	Pallis, Alexander	Tatoi, Aigburth Drive
97	Paterson, Andrew M., Professor of Anatomy	2 Ivanhoe Road
174	Patterson, William, S.	11 Fulwood Park
118	Paul, Edward Jr.	Teignton, Aigburth Vale
86	Perkins, Hugh, JP, DL	7 Fulwood Park
190	Pferdmenges, William, Merchant	4 Livingston Drive
257	Place, Mrs Lucy	9 Pelham Grove
23	Pollok, Thomas, Rope Maker	33 Marmion Road
211	Porter, George, Builder & Contractor	99 Lark Lane
61	Prager, Louis	Normanton Grove, Langham Ave
92	Pretty, Geo	82 Lark Lane
161	Pritchard, Frederick	3 Bertram Road
62	Purgold, Emile	10 Alexandra Drive
93	Radford, A. S.	5 Normanton Avenue
151	Radforth, H. A.	158 Aigburth Road
183	Ralli Costi C., Merchant	28 Linnet Lane
36	Ralli, Geo C.	Iona, Linnet Lane, Sefton Park
20	Rankin, John	6 Livingston Drive
132	Rathbone, George	Ivy Lodge, Aigburth
74	Rathbone, Hugh R., Merchant	Oakburth, Aigburth
17	Rayner, Lloyd	Hargreaves Road, Sefton Park
112	Read & Co.	16 Lark Lane
242	Relf, John	Northwood, St Michael's
206	Rensburg, Henry E.	12 Ivanhoe Road
130	Ritson, Hunter, Grocer, Provision Merchant	14 Lark Lane & Aigburth Road
124	Rittner, G. S., Merchant	The Shrubbery, Aigburth Road
176	Roberts, A. L.	5 Waverley Road, Sefton Park
95	Roberts, W. G., Copper Merchant	14 St Michael's Road

108	Robertson, G. H. F.	51 Parkfield Road, Sefton Park
256	Rome, Thomas	The Lings, Livingston Drive South
234	Rooke, Louis F.	14 Ivanhoe Road
209	Rosenheim, Felix, Merchant	6 Parkfield Road
19	Roxburgh, John	Rowallan, Aigburth Drive
255	Sanxay, E. C.	2 Linnet Lane
76	Sawden, Alfred, Pharmaceutical Chemist	28 Lark Lane, Sefton Park
40	Servaes, Julius	Holly Lea, Livingston Drive
5	Shaw, Frank	Ellerslie, Aigburth Drive
232	Sidley, Frank H., Stationer	96 Lark Lane
39	Sing, Joshua	Kelton, Aigburth
89	Smith, Andrew T. Jr	5 Hargreaves Road
239	Smith, H. W.	20 Ullet Road
224	Smith, Mrs. E. B.	14 Bertram Road
173	Smith, Radcliffe W., Solicitor	3 Normanton Avenue, Sefton Park
221	Smith, Samuel, MP	Carleton, Princes Park
223	Smith & Son, Grocers, Provision Merchants	110 Aigburth Road
146	Smith, Thomas, Fish, Game, Poultry	178 Aigburth Road
68	Smith's Pharmacy (John), Chemist	164 Aigburth Road
65	Solomon, Louis, Merchant	Claremont, 18 Ullet Road
25	Springmann, J. H.	5 Livingston Drive North
14	Steel, Arthur J.	Beresford House, Aigburth Drive
16	Steeves, G. Walter, MD	3 Parkfield Road
105	Steinmann, R. Sr.	7 Linnet Lane
82	Steinmann, Rudolf Jr., Merchant and Agent	Normanton, Normanton Avenue
63	Stuart, T. W.	7 Livingston Drive
170	Taplin, Alfred Betts, Physician	Ivanhoe Road, Sefton Park
201	Taylor, W. Ernest, Solicitor	6 Waverley Road, Sefton Park
177	Ten Bosch, J. M	5 Alexandra Drive
50	Thomas, Llewelyn	44 Parkfield Road
48	Thomas, Robert (Smith), Chemist	129 Lark Lane, Sefton Park
33	Thomson, Wm., Steamship Owner	Glendavagh, Livingston Drive South
158	Turner, Frederick	15 Bertram Road, Sefton Park
237	Turner, Robert	5 Parkfield Road, Princes Park
6	Unsworth's Ltd, Car Proprietors	100 Lark Lane, Sefton Park
233	Unsworth's Ltd, Car Proprietors	26 Ullet Road
1	Unsworth's Ltd, Car Proprietors	Park Lane Mews
210	Walker, John & Son Ltd, Wine Merchants	73 Lark Lane
41	Waring, S. J.	Palmyra, 5 Aigburth Vale
8	Warr, Augustus F.	5 Alexandra Drive, Princes Park
202	Whitney, Col. C.A., V.D.	Grange, Fulwood Park
119	Wilkinson, J. L.	34 Parkfield Road
243	Williamson, J. Guthrie	Otterspool, Aigburth
160	Williamson, R. P.	Holly Bank, St Michael's Road
154	Williamson, W. S., Corn Broker	18 Ivanhoe Road
56	Wilson, George, Ad Head	Netherwater, Aigburth Road
73	Wilson, John, Merchant (Wilson Meyer & Co.)	Livingston Drive North, Sefton Park
180	Wilson, T. Wadsworth, Baker & Confectioner	13 Lark Lane

181	Windsor, Edwin	Ballrath, Linnet Lane
227	Woodall, Alfred	25 Fulwood Park
113	Wooler, Richard	Aigburth Road
3	Wright, J. D., B.A., MB, B.Ch.	67 Parkfield Road, Princes Park
102	Wylie, Walter	9 Waverley Road

Public Call Offices

6	Robert Unsworth	100 Lark Lane
1	Joseph Crone	Lark Lane Mews

St. Michael-in-the-Hamlet Church. KF

List of Interviewees, 1980-81

I conducted all the interviews and recorded them either on tape or by longhand. The tapes and notes were transcribed between 1980-1983 and a draft typescript was prepared on my Olympia portable typewriter. The tapes were sadly lost as I moved between various houses in the UK, California and New Zealand over the past four decades. A flooded basement was one factor.

I Part II Interviewees, 1980-81

Mrs. Margaret McLean, née Richardson b. Bickerton Street 1887, worked in a hat shop, service as live-in kitchen maid, married 1907, widowed 1933, six children, harmonica player.

Working on the Lane

1. Miss Edwards, cook at Stevenson's bakery, opened 1868.
2. Mr. Carmichael, owner/manager of Glendinning's fish and poultry, opened 1876.
3. Mr. Harry Tonkiss, florist, family on Lane since 1911.
4. Mrs. Louise (Lulu) Williams, née Tonkiss, florist.
5. Mrs. Edith Barnard, florist, began with Tonkiss's.
6. Mr. Tony Hutchinson, Charlett's Funeral Services.
7. Mr. John Hogg, dairyman, great-grandson of founder of John Hogg & Sons, started 1872.
8. Mr. E. Callister, quality upholsterer, on Lane since 1963.
9. Mr. Sam (or Harry?) Corkill, garage owner and former Post Office employee, in area since 1930s.
10. Mr. G. J. Williams, chemist, moved to Lane in 1969, took over from Mr. Perkins, who had worked there 43 years.
11. Mr. Bob Smyth, furniture remover, set up business in 1930s, did apprenticeship at Rushton's on the Lane.
12. Mr. C. E. Sexton, plumber and builder, 13 Hadassah Grove.
13. Mr. Jim Duffy, butcher.
14. Mrs. Parry, The Sunshine Café, on the Lane for two years.

15. Mr. E. Low, Turn of the Century antique shop, opened 1975. Worked in Australia 1963-72 in nursing and social services.
16. Mrs. Annie Beattie, attendant, Pelham launderette.
17. Lesley Phillips, bookshop. Open on the Lane 18 months.
18. Mrs. Pauline Butterfield, Butterfield's Fruiterer and Greengrocer. Moved to the Lane 1970.
19. Paul Robinson, hairdresser at Paul's on the Lane for 14 years.
20. Barry Hayden, hairdresser.
21. Keith Haggis, founder of Keith's Wine Bar, opened 1978.
22. Mrs. Ruth Heague, manageress of the Masonic Pub, husband Fred.
23. Danny Kay, manager of the Albert Hotel, moved from Wigan to the Lane in 1974.
24. Derek Murray, Larks in the Park founder, antique shop.
25. Kevin Hessey, shoe repairs.
26. L'Alouette, French restaurant. Vivienne Wilson, Arthur Wilson, Michael Morley, Beatrice Morley.

Residents

27. Julian Kenyon, former surgeon now working in alternative medicine, trained in acupuncture, moved to the area 1974. Lives Alexandra Drive, business premises on Aigburth Drive.
28. Mr. James (Jim), mechanical engineer, and Mrs. Jane Baxter, honorary secretary of Lark Lane Traders' Association.
29. Helen Prescott, director of arts association and editor of *Creative Mind*, launched December 1978.
30. Mr. David Gibbon, building surveyor, b. Edinburgh. Living in 19 Hadassah Grove since 1977. Active member of Lark Lane Community Association.
31. Mr. Alan Hoyte, member of Hesketh Street Housing Cooperative, formed 1977.
32. Rev. A. Thomas, vicar of Christ Church, Linnet Lane.

Six Older Residents

33. Mr. Sam Evans, b. Bickerton Street 1902, gas fitter for 57 years, with Mrs. Mary Evans.

34. Miss Iva Jones, b. Hesketh Street, lives Lucerne St., domestic servant and factory worker (Plesseys and Thorntons).
35. Mrs. Dora Ince, clerk and mother.
36. Dr. Grace Gillespie, medical doctor, and Mr. Bryce Gillespie, teacher and pilot.

Growing up in the Big Houses

37. Miss Joan Carey, b. Alexandra Drive, daughter of university registrar; games mistress.
38. Miss K. Rutherford, Parkfield Rd., daughter of Lord Mayor; secretary of LP Needlework Guild, jigsaw puzzle maker.
39. Mr. F. J. Camenisch, solicitor, grandfather lived 8 Aigburth Drive.
40. Miss Anne Brocklehurst, WW2 ambulance driver and honorary secretary, Voluntary Society for the Blind.
41. Mrs. Jessie de Larrinaga, née Hands, b. Gambier Terrace. Shipowners, living Livingston Drive.
42. Miss Doris Forster, governess and voluntary social worker.
43. The Family of Frank Charles Minoprio. Letter.

Institutions

44. Mr. Griffiths, Headmaster, St. Michael-in-the-Hamlet School.
45. Mr. J.F.A. Roderick, Headmaster, St. Charles Catholic Primary School.
46. Miss E. M. Jellis, Principal, Shorefields Comprehensive School.
47. Mrs. Collins, Headmistress, Aigburth Vale Comprehensive School.
48. Mrs. Owen, Librarian, Sefton Park Branch, Liverpool Public Library.
49. Post Office and Sorting Office.
50. Police Station and Fire Station.
51. Telephone Exchange.
52. Churches.
53. Sefton Park and Community Life.

Online Contributors, 2019-2021

Part II Interview 2 Paul Mooney; 3 Jennifer Robinson; 4 Steve Tonkiss, Gareth Williams; 11 John Smyth; 13 Paul Banks; 17 Pip Schofield; 18 Sharon Jackson, née Butterfield; 20 Lynn Bligh McCann; 24 Denyze Alleyne-Johnson; 26 Janisimo Jones; 28 Andrew Butterfield; 37 Lorna Moffatt, Jane Dow, Irene Vickers, Susan Milce Quinlan (née Milce), Shirley Ann Cheyne; 41 Geoff Edwards; 48 Margaret McDermott, 49 Sian Poynton

Part III Growing Up Around the Lane

1. Bickerton Street - Keith Draper, Jean Wall, née Batten, Joan Major, née Batten, Dave Turton, Heath Gar, Lynn Brown Lawrenson, Michael Smith, Sue O'Hagan

2. Hesketh Street - Sharon McGovern, née Costain/Luby

3. Lark Lane - Judy Murphy, née Halpin, Carole Rich, née Johnson, Geraldine Kaeo, Kin Hau, Andrew Butterfield

4. Leda Grove - Paul Banks, Barrie Carlson, Diane Clark, Keith Draper, John Jones, Kay Jones, Harry Letman, Bev Magee, Kathy Wilkinson

5. Little Parkfield Road - Graeme Edwards, Elaine Dutton, Mary Russell, née Willingham, Hazel Partington, née Smith, Wendi Surtees-Smith, Philippa Mulberry, née Smith

6. Marmion Road - Marianne Ruscoe

7. Pelham Grove - Peter Vernon, Caroline Oates

8. Princes View - Paul Banks

9. Sefton Grove - Eileen Goncalves, née Powell, Alan C. Powell, Tom Powell, Helena Paxton, née Goncalves, Robert (Bob) Stephen White, Beryl Byrne, née White

10. Siddeley Street - Lindsay Rimmer, née Walsh, Lynne Bywater, Marg Hibbert, née Kelly

Part IV Global Village: the Lane Today, 2020

Marianne Ruscoe, Alex Corina, Sally Ayres, Lynn Brown Lawrenson, Caroline Oates

Four Women on the Lane, 1981. TW

Illustration Credits

There is something miraculous about a 40-year project, especially one that involves collaboration. I owe a special debt to Tom Wood, both for his initial dedication to the project in 1980-81, and for his renewed time and efforts in 2019-20 in retrieving and preparing this stunning selection of his original work. Tom and Bryan Biggs urged the inclusion of historic photographs, which were painstakingly sourced from the Liverpool Record Office by Tom's assistant, Richard Millichap.

Grateful thanks to the Liverpool Record Office for their assistance, and to Caroline Oates, Dave Turton, Alex Corina and Helena and Tony Paxton for their contributions of photographs, aerial photographs, and other artworks.

Thanks to all who have graciously allowed us to use precious family photographs. Sharing family stories in the collective framework of a book helps to revitalise city streets by peopling them with those who lived here earlier. The Lark Lane/Sefton Park/St. Michael's Hamlet area deserves to become more widely known as one of Liverpool's most exciting and varied heritage districts.

Paul Banks:	223
Jane Baxter:	101, 102, 103
Bryan Biggs:	106
Beryl Byrne:	178, 235
Lynne Bywater:	238
Barrie Carlson:	206
Alex Corina:	241-2, 245, 246, 247, 249
KF:	iv, 36, 86, 97, 115, 121, 160, 162, 180, 252, 262, 270, 285
David Gibbon:	111
Sharon Jackson:	75
Janisimo Jones:	95
Holly Lodge:	126
Lynn Brown Lawrenson:	186, 187

Robert Lewis:	26
Liverpool Record Office:	xiii-xiv, 4, 5, 9, 10, 12, 13, 15-16, 17, 27, 30, 43, 52, 119, 120, 134, 136, 138, 139, 144, 164, 197, 224, 229, 263
Sharon McGovern:	196
Girija Madhavan:	123
Joan Major:	178
Judy Murphy:	199
National Museums Liverpool:	141
Caroline Oates:	front cover, vii, 194, 208, 217, 225
Sue O'Hagan:	192
Alexandra Kopp:	35
Hazel Partington, Wendi Surtees-Smith, Philippa Mulberry:	210
Helena Paxton:	166
Helena Paxton and Tony Paxton:	v-vi, ix
Tony Paxton:	232
Carole Rich:	157, 202
Alan Powell:	228
Tom Powell:	226
Helen Prescott:	105
Carole Rich:	202
Helen Seymour:	248
Michael Smith:	188, 189, 191
John Smyth:	54, 55
Dave Turton:	22, 170, 182, 184
Peter Vernon:	218
Gareth Williams and Steve Tonkiss:	38, 40, 41, 42
Tom Wood:	25, 37, 47, 53, 59, 62, 63, 65, 67, 69, 70, 72, 76, 77, 78, 81, 82, 84, 87, 88, 89, 94, 117, 153, 168, 169, 203, 275, 281, 282
Yale University Press:	289

Bibliography

In 1980-81 I took a year's unpaid leave from University College London and moved into 16 Pelham Grove with my husband and our eight-year old daughter Rebecca. My plan was to work on a research project studying the American years of Berlin-born Expressionist artist George Grosz (1893-1959). But within a month of moving into Pelham Grove, I became caught up in the special magic of the Lark Lane area. I wanted to record its stories! After a struggle I decided on 3 days a week for Grosz, and 2 days for Lark Lane.

To provide a visual complement to my story-collecting and to help me keep on track, I also commissioned a photographic study of its people and places by Tom Wood, after seeing some of his work at a local exhibition. In August 1983 my family moved to Berkeley, California. The unfinished People of the Lane dropped out of sight until October 2019, when I revisited Liverpool for the first time.

Written Records

Although the book is based mainly on interviews with local residents between 1980-1983, I also made extensive use of published and unpublished written records. Sincere thanks to the staff of the Liverpool Record Office [LRO] for their help during those years.

I Maps:

a. 1769 'Plan of Toxteth Park.' The area is wholly rural, and the lines along which Aigburth Road and Lark Lane will later be made are marked as field boundaries.

b. 1847 'Plan of the Township of Toxteth Park in the Parish of Walton-on-the-Hill in the County of Lancaster.' Lark Lane and Linnet Lane are marked in, and a small cluster of houses are shown around an unnamed lane now known as Hadassah Grove.

Until 1895 the city boundary ran along Ullet Road.

II Books and pamphlets:

Alfred Booth, 1834-1914. Commemorative addresses. Privately printed, Liverpool 1914.
Elizabeth Bradburn, *Dr. Dora Esther Yates. An Appreciation.* Liverpool 1974.
Elfreda H. C. Cotton, 'Reminiscences of the Twentieth Century in Relation to the Civic Life of Liverpool' (1980). Typescript of tape recording in LRO.
George Chandler, *Liverpool.* London 1957.
M. Kay Flavell, 'The Enlightened Reader and the New Industrial Towns: A Study of the Liverpool Library, 1758-1790', *British Journal of Eighteenth Century Studies,* 8 (1985), 17-35.
Doris Forster, *Dr. John Watson,* 1859-1907. Privately printed, for records of Sefton Park Church, Liverpool 1978.
Kelly's (Gore's) Street Director of Liverpool, 1880 onwards.
Robert Griffiths, *History of the Royal and Ancient Park of Toxteth.* Liverpool 1907.
Thomas Kelly, *For Advancement of Learning.* The University of Liverpool, 1881-1981. Liverpool 1981.
James Laver, *Museum Piece, or the Education of an Iconographer.* London 1963.
Liverpool Conservation Areas. Liverpool Heritage Bureau, City Planning Dept., 1979.
Thomas Lloyd-Jones, *Street Names of Liverpool.* Liverpool 1981.
Merseyside in Crisis. Merseyside Socialist Research Group, Liverpool 1980.
Ramsay Muir, *History of Liverpool.* Liverpool 1907. *"An Autobiography and Some Essays".* London 1943.
Michael Mahony, *Ways and Byways in Liverpool.* Liverpool 1936.
B. G. Orchard, *Liverpool's Legion of Honour.* Birkenhead 1893.
Sir James Picton, *Memorials of Liverpool.* 2 vols, London 1875.
W. T. Pike, *Liverpool and Birkenhead in the 20th Century.* Contemporary Biographies, Liverpool 1911.
Stanley Roberts, 'The Liverpool Telephone Area Story'. From the *Journal of the Liverpool Telephone Area.* And private correspondence re the Lark Lane Exchange.
John D. Robertson, 'The History of the Liverpool Fire Brigade'. Mimeographed essay, Liverpool 1983.
Fritz Spiegl, *Genuine Liverpool Street Songs.* Liverpool 1966.
David Wainwright, *Liverpool Gentlemen. A History of Liverpool College.* London 1960.
John Willett, *Art in a City.* London 1967.
Peter Howell Williams, *Liverpolitans. A Miscellany of People and Places.* Merseyside Civic Society 1971.
Dora E. Yates, *My Gypsy Days. Recollections of a Romani Rawnie.* Phoenix House, London 1953.

Private records

Records of St. Michael–in-the-Hamlet School, St. Charles Catholic Primary School, Aigburth Vale Comprehensive School and Shorefields Comprehensive School.
Private records of Sefton Park Presbyterian Church.
Reports of St. Michael's and Lark Lane Community Association, 1976-1980.

2020 – Additional reading

Johanna Alberti. Eleanor *Rathbone*. SAGE Publications, London 1996.
Sven Beckert, *Empire of Cotton. A Global History*, Vintage Books, 2014.
John Belchem, ed., *Liverpool 800. Culture, Character and History*. Liverpool University Press, 2006. This exceptional volume describes itself as 'a form of urban biography concerned with continuity and change in Liverpool culture and character, image and identity, examining the complex and contested ways in which Liverpool has projected itself and how it has been portrayed by others.' The present work shares a similar interest in observing continuity and change on a smaller scale, recording visual and spoken moments in a Liverpool urban village as experienced by several generations of adults, children, and older members.
John Belchem and Bryan Biggs, eds. *Liverpool: City of Radicals*. Liverpool University Press, 2011.
Bryan Biggs, (ed.) *Tricia Porter: Liverpool Photographs, 1972-74*. The Bluecoat, 2015.
Eavan Boland, *A Poet's Dublin*. Edited by Paula Meehan and Jody Allen Randolph. With photographs by Eavan Boland. W.W.Norton, 2016.
Ann Breen and Dick Rigby, *Waterfronts. Cities Reclaim their Edge*. McGraw-Hill, Inc., 1994.
Cities for the 21st Century. Organisation for Economic Co-operation and Development, 1994.
Albert Fein, (ed.) *Landscape into Cityscape. Frederick Law Olmsted's Plans for a Greater New York City*. Van Nostrand Reinhold Company, 1981.
From Pitt Street to Granby. Writing on the Wall, co-directed by Mike Morris and Madeline Heneghan. Introduction by Mike Boyle, Tony Wailey, Madeline Heneghan, Toxteth Library, 2018.
Michael Heseltine, *Where There's a Will*. Hutchinson, London 1987.
Francis R. Kowsky, *Country, Park and City. The Architecture and Life of Calvert Vaux*. Oxford University Press, 1998.
Ursula K. LeGuin and Roger Dorband, *Blue Moon over Thurman Street*. NewSage Press, 1993.
Charles Montgomery, *Happy City. Transforming Our Lives Through Urban Design*. Penguin Random House, 2013.
Dan Morgan, *Merchants of Grain*. I universe, 2000.
Susan Pedersen, *Eleanor Rathbone and the Politics of Conscience*. Yale University Press, 2004.

Joseph Sharples, *Liverpool. Pevsner Architectural Guides.* Yale University Press, 2004.
Fran Tonkiss, *Cities by Design. The Social Life of Urban Form.* Polity, London 2013.
Calvert Vaux, *Villas and Cottages* (1864). Dover Publications, New York, 1970.
Martin Wainwright,' Michael Heseltine is given the Freedom of Liverpool'
    The Guardian, 13 March 2012.
Ai Weiwei, *Humanity.* Edited and with an introduction by Larry Warsh.
    Princeton University Press, 2018.

Off to a game of tennis in Sefton Park. TW

George (Docker) Roberts with his dog Gypsy (aka Gipfast) in his garage in Hesketh Street, next to Hadassah Grove. Docker was a skilled mechanic and a lover of digestive biscuits. Joe Williams recalls: 'I worked with him. He taught me how to weld and spray cars.' TW

About the Photographer

Thomas "Tom" Wood was born in 1951 in the west of Ireland, moving to England with his family in 1955. He studied Fine Art and experimental film at Leicester Polytechnic from 1973-1976, and then began to study photography on his own. In 1978 he moved to Merseyside. There he soon became well known as 'the photie-man' for his street photography, working on the streets, in pubs and clubs, markets and football grounds. His work on Lark Lane dates from his early days in Liverpool. In 2003 he moved to North Wales, to continue a long time exploration of landscape.

An early influence was Ronald Blythe's *Akenfield. Portrait of an English Village* (1969). 'I was working nights in a car factory when I read it. I still buy it whenever I see it and give it away to people,' he says.

Wood was awarded the Prix Dialogue de l'Humanité at the Rencontres d'Arles in 2002. In 2014 he was the subject of a programme in the BBC4 documentary series *What Do Artists Do All Day?* A major British show, *Men and Women*, was at the Photographers' Gallery in London in 2012, and in 2013 a full UK retrospective was held at the National Media Museum in Bradford. His exhibition *'Tom Wood: Britain in the 80s'* was held at the Multimedia Art Museum, Moscow in 2017.

His first book and most famous series, *Looking for Love* (1989) shows people up close and personal at the Chelsea Reach disco club in New Brighton, Merseyside. Further books include *All Zones Off Peak* (1998) based on his 18 years of riding the buses of Liverpool and *People* (1999). The retrospective book *Photie Man* (2005) was made in collaboration with Irish artist Padraig Timoney. It included several of the Lark Lane images.

Tom Wood self portrait, c.1979.

About the Author

Kay Flavell is a poet, scholar and story collector. Born in 1943, she grew up on a pig farm in Dunedin, New Zealand. Her Flavell, Murray, Harrison and Crago great-grandparents emigrated to New Zealand between the 1850s and 1870s from Birmingham, the Scottish Borders, Dundalk, and Truro. She has a B.A. in English and German from the University of Otago, a Ph.D. in German from the University of London, and an M.A. in Museum Studies and Cultural Policy from Monash University, Melbourne.

She taught in the Dept. of German at University College London from 1969-81, held a Senior Research Fellowship at the University of Liverpool from 1981-83, and taught in German and Critical Theory at the University of California at Davis between 1984 and 2001. She lives in an old farmhouse in Vallejo, California.

She is founder and director of New Pacific Studio, www.newpacificstudio.org, a residency programme for artists, writers, and environmentalists.

Her books include *George Grosz. A Biography* (Yale University Press, 1988), *Moon over the Pacific. A poet's travel diary* (Steele Roberts, 2005), and *Living in Kaiparoro* (2008).

Ancient Chapel of Toxteth. KF

Kay Flavell, *Echo*, August 1983.

About the Designer

Tracy Dean, born in Saskatchewan, Canada, is a designer, foodie, and gardener. She graduated from the California College of the Arts in San Francisco in the early 90s. She currently runs Design Site, a branding and web site design company in Berkeley.

Design Site was founded in 1993, and while a lot has changed since then, she has stayed true to the same principles:

Good design is timeless.
Good design is transparent to the message.
Good design conveys quality, integrity and honesty.

Tracy Dean

Acknowledgements

People of the Lane is a collaborative project dedicated to the people of the district. My deepest thanks to all our interviewees and online contributors mentioned above (pp. 269-273) for sharing their stories. I take responsibility for all errors and omissions.

Thanks to Tom Wood for permission to include his photographs, and to Bryan Biggs for his contributions. I am also immensely grateful to Tom for his assembling of historical photographs, with the assistance of Richard Millichap.

Thanks to Caroline Oates, Dave Turton, Alex Corina and Tony and Helena Paxton for being so helpful at every stage of the book journey from 2019-2021, and for the use of their artwork. Helena Paxton has also been a model editor, skillful, patient and always encouraging. Tracy Dean of Design Site has been a joy to work with.

Jan Grace at the Liverpool Record Office has offered steady encouragement. Thanks to Michael March for his valuable help. Phil Bannister, Debbie Fairfield, Terri Langley and Carol Davis have also contributed in different ways.

Finally, thanks to the Lark Lane Neighbourhood Association for their encouragement. I hope that book sales will augment their funds and be used for the greater good of the whole community.

Victorian bandstand in Sefton Park. KF

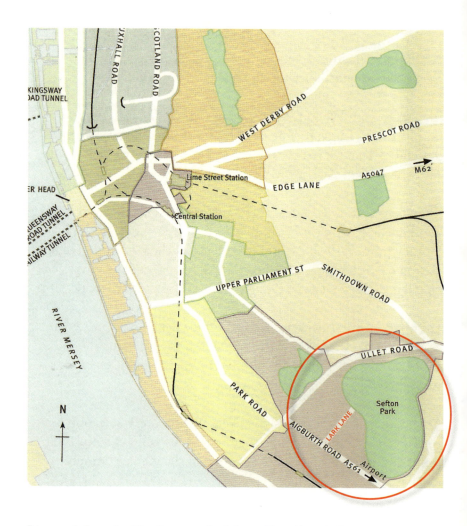

Liverpool, from the City Centre to Lark Lane. From Joseph Sharples, *Liverpool*. Yale University Press, 2004.